About Taslima

Taslima Nasreen is a physician, writer, feminist, human rights activist and a secular humanist. She was born in a conservative Muslim environment but still became independent in thought and action. She quit her government job as a doctor, as she was not allowed to publish her writings. Her first documentary novel, *Lajja*, that won accolades the world over, created a furore and the religious fundamentalists began demanding her head. Her books were banned and she was banished from Bangladesh. Her next venture, *Dwikhandito* that was published as *Ka* in India, met similar fate—it was banned by the West Bengal Government on the ground that it hurt the sentiments of a community and created communal division. Later, Calcutta High Court lifted the ban.

Her books have been translated in 30 languages including English and French. After being banished from Bangladesh, she lived in western countries, and then in Kolkata for three years. But as fundamentalist groups targeted her, the government of West Bengal refused to let her stay in Bengal. The Indian Government too refused to renew her visa. She had to go back to Europe after living under house arrest for almost seven-and-a-half months. Taslima, however, waits eagerly for the day when she will be allowed to live in either Bangladesh or West Bengal.

Notwithstanding criticism, Taslima has received many awards too. These include Shakharov Prize from European Parliament for free thinking, UNESCO prize for Tolerance and Peace, Kurt Tukholsky Prize from Sweden, Arwin Fischer Prize from Germany, Simone de Beauvoir Prize of France, Feminist Press Prize from the US and Honorary Doctorate from Guest University of Belgium and American University of Paris.

Taslima Nasreen
No Country for Women

Taslima Nasreen
No Country for Women

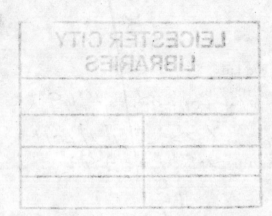

Vitasta

Vitasta Publishing Pvt. Ltd.
New Delhi

Published by
Sudesh K Verma for
Vitasta Publishing Pvt. Ltd.
2/15, Ansari Road, Daryaganj,
New Delhi - 110 002

ISBN 978-81-89766-64-1
© Taslima Nasreen 2010

Reprint 2010

The views and opinions expressed in this book are the author's own. She is solely responsible for the facts and authenticity of the quotes and sources used for this work. The publisher in no way is liable for the same.

Translated by Diptendra Raychaudhuri and others
Cover Design and Layout by Vitasta Publishing Pvt. Ltd.
Printed by Vits Press, New Delhi

Contents

viii

Publisher's Note

This book was originally published in Bangla in 2007 by the name of *Narir Kono Desh Nei*. The present translation in English is an attempt to bring her powerful views on feminism and women liberation before that section of the society which is influential and forms part of the opinion makers. Many places, the essays may appear dated, but these should be seen in the context they were written.

Preface

The articles published in different newspapers are now here. I believe that women have no country. If country means security, if country means freedom, then women obviously do not have any country. Women do not get freedom anywhere in the world. They are not safe—this is realized when one reads the daily newspapers. Many of the articles in this book are reactions on everyday stories of women's unsecured life. I am trying to frame the small segment of time that I am witnessing. I have a 'courageous' dream that the dark pictures which are shown now would be bright in future. Yet, I never forget that I am one of the million oppressed women on this earth. Through my story, I wish to tell the world how we (women) are living.

Taslima Nasreen

Men Enjoy Rights, Women Shoulder Responsibilities

As citizens of a state, women do not enjoy the same status as men do. That they should enjoy it, is no new proposition. It was emphasized for ages, by all righteous persons advocating faith and equality, and truth. By citing heaps of facts and theories, they have shown what was the condition of women in the past, where it has reached through evolution, and the yawning gap that still exists between where they are and where they should be.

It is not that the women are victims of deprivation only in the third world countries. For centuries, even in the first world countries, people had no idea that besides being mothers, the women were human beings too. They had always been viewed as something insignificant, not as equal citizens. The word 'citizen' is derived from the term 'city'. Once, each city was a state. One thousand and five hundred cities scattered on the edges of the Mediterranean Sea—Plato had humorously described them as 'frogs around the pond'—once constituted the then Greece. There the concept of democracy originated two thousand and five hundred years ago. Even in that democracy, the status of citizenship was enjoyed by a very chosen few, like those who were at the helm of affairs in the governance, who spread consciousness about politics, a few aristocrats. Children, women and slaves were deprived from citizenship.

Citizenship, civil rights and all those concepts have undergone a gradual uplift. With the expansion of the Roman Empire, the concept of citizenship became more extensive and profound. That was necessary for the protection of the empire. The basic tenets of citizenship included inculcation of civic awareness and commitment to protection of the state, dedication to the altar of duty, labour, discipline, patriotism and love for fellow citizen. Everyone in the empire got the right to citizenship. It was enshrined in writing and made legal. Excellent! But two classes were deprived of the privilege of becoming citizen: women and the outcasts.

From 16th Century onwards, the responsibility of one group spilled over on the shoulders of the other. The citizens were entrusted with a host of duties to perform, but what about the state's duty towards its citizens? The state was obliged to ensure a citizen's personal security and the security of his family and belongings. The impact of the thoughts of French philosophers on the duties and responsibility of the state and rights of a citizen was so immense that a strange incident like the French Revolution took place. The law that enshrined the rights of a man was enacted. At the same time, the wind of change began to blow in America and other developed nations. It witnessed the freedom movement, establishment of democracy and the framing of the constitution that guaranteed equal rights; but slavery, imperialism, colonialism, male chauvinism continued in full steam. There was no change in the rights and dignity of the black, the poor and the women.

The males in this way passed their own rights as human rights. Not a single revolution, or constitution, or law on earth said a single word in favour of women. Even great philosophers and revolutionaries lacked the mind that considered women too as human beings. The rights were all for the men; freedom of speech, right to vote, right to contest elections, right to freedom were all designed keeping men in mind. Women were allotted responsibilities—responsibilities such as looking after the household, to arrange for men's comfort, to beget and rear children. Centuries after centuries, women were confined into closed walls. Meanwhile, the so-called democracy had started glowing, pomp and grandeur, was being added to it; but freedom and rights became the monopoly of males only. Amazingly, nobody uttered a single word for women's rights. One or two men had spoken for women; but ultimately women had to come to the forefront and shed blood to establish their own rights. In Europe and other western countries, women have been able to battle successfully against the exploitation of men, and earned the right to vote. But success of European women does not necessarily mean that all women of the rest of the world earned this particular right. Even in this 21st Century, women are not allowed to cast their votes in many countries of the world. They are still victims of discrimination and deprived from their rights in every field such as politics, education, economy and health.

How did the pioneers of the anti-colonial nationalist movement in India look upon women? To convince the world, during the conflict with the colonial forces, about the superiority to the West in terms of purity, the nationalist leaders of this subcontinent ended up relegating women further to the prison of narrow, domestic world. Though Indian culture was the culture that crushed women's rights, the nationalist leaders entrusted women with the task of safeguarding Indian culture. During the period between late 19th and the beginning of the 20th Century, lots of books were written to indicate that the actual status of women was within her household. The outside world belonged to men. The outside world called for courage, strength; it demanded stamina, struggle; it was a world of war, of politics; it befitted men, not women. Women were fragile, frail and vulnerable. They were cowards, foolish. So, they were expected to dedicate themselves to their domestic duties that demanded self-sacrifice and self-oblivion. Slightest deviation from it was unthinkable. At the same time, men were essentially embodiment of two virtues: self-reliance and self-esteem. The presence of these two virtues in a woman was believed to bring about erosion of family and social structures.

When they talked about education of women, they meant churning out ideal wives and ideal mothers. The book published in 1942 entitled *Nari Dharma Shiksha* was an attempt to teach the spirit of discipline, cleanliness, politeness and obedience.

The book sported the photographs of an ideal woman. One picture depicted a woman busy in a neatly arranged kitchen, the second, a woman in a well-decorated drawing room reading a book entitled, *Duties of Women*, and the third, in a similar room, fondling a baby. The book also talks of the guidelines to be religiously followed by women:

- Pray to God after rising and before going to bed
- Rise before sunrise and if you fail to do so, observe fasting as a penance
- After bath, offer prayer to Sun God
- Chant *Hare Ram* 500 times
- Remember God once in every hour
- Touch the feet of elders and take dust to show your respect to them
- Never lose temper
- Worship God
- Never display your discontent over anything
- If your eyes catch the attention of a man other than your husband, think of God at once
- Never criticize others
- While treating someone with food, don't dupe him
- Never be ruthless
- Never hurt others
- Always tell the truth
- Don't hide anything
- If you perchance, flout the norms, chant *Hare Ram* 108 times

All these dictates were firmly rooted in the cult of overstretched nationalism, religion and male chauvinism. Women were insinuated into the worlds of God, husband and home. Indian women must be the symbol of Indian traditions and culture, but they should not be entitled to full citizenship and rights. Their attempt to participate in India's social, economic and political arena should be thwarted by all means. This was a fact. The men, educated with western thoughts and ideologies, became all-in-all, thanks to their knowledge and efficiency. They armed themselves with the language and culture of their foreign rulers, and then challenged the latter. So far so good! But what was expected from them as believers in equality was that they would emancipate women from the holes of domestic confines, but they did just the opposite.

During the period from 1917 to 1940, debates and discussion, albeit milder in form than what was going on in Europe for the acquisition of women's right to vote, were carried out in India as well. The right to vote is a citizen's basic political right, yet in India, this right was denied by both Hindu and Muslim nationalist leaders. They rent the sky with the clamour that women's right to vote would destroy the very fabric of family and the purity of the purdah system. Womanhood and citizenship, they claimed, could never meet.

In the early 1930s, the women were divided into—what was desirable—reservation of seats for women or universal adult franchise. The political leaders got themselves embroiled in a controversy over the issue. The debates continued for a pretty long time. Amidst this, one fine morning of September 1932, some Congress leaders including Gandhiji signed the Poona Pact and arranged for reservation of seats for women in the Hindu areas. Thus, they had made a compromise that had sought to strangle the United Movement of Women from all communities and religious sects for their right to vote.

Till the anti-British movement gathered momentum, the feminists in India, inspired by the English and the Irish feminists, took to the streets to demand their right to vote. But soon this movement was nipped in the bud by the wings of the nationalist movement. The countrymen were in deep longing for the test of freedom. The national consciousness was increasingly being fed on the ancient, obsolete concept patronized by the male-dominated society that looked down upon women as slaves. Though in that period some women's organizations existed in a scattered way, they all joined the mainstream of national movement. When the question of the right to vote arose, Sarojini Naidu, Begum Shahnawaz, Radharani Subbarian and many others began to mumble that women were capable of playing a role in politics and cast vote even after performing their household duties. This will not harm their feminine virtues or virginity. If they attain political awareness, they can nurture their children into ideal human beings. To avoid being misunderstood, those women leaders clarified their stance by declaring that they were not feminists and, unlike their counterparts in the West, they were not in favour of waging a gender war. Moreover, in their opinion, India never required any feminist movement because in India, men and women were accustomed to cooperate with each other in every walk of life! Some upper class, educated, solvent, privileged women had most pitifully forgotten the condition of the majority of women, the majority languishing in deprivation, distress, illiteracy, repression, neglect and disgrace. With the Independence and Partition of the country, the women population was also split into groups. Their identity no longer remained 'women' only. They were divided into two groups, majority and minority. They became instruments for propping up the division of the country based on pure religions. In India, there had been a great possibility of women's liberation movement. But it was crushed in the hands of national leaders. This gave a golden opportunity to the uneducated and impatient Islamic men, who deprived their women counterparts of the basic human rights, security and justice which had been recognised by Indian democracy. The Shah Bano case was a striking example of how the communal state power was giving indulgence to this.

In 1934, the demand of equality, the demand of ending discrimination against women in inheritance, marriage and guardianship of children were raised in all-India women's meet. Those demands remained just demands. Even now these demands are like 'untouchables'. Even the secular people of India are scared to support the demands of reforming or abolishing Muslim Personal Law. Does democracy not entail that there should be a uniform civil code ensuring equality between men and women? If religious laws violate human rights, destroy individual freedom, then what good is served by keeping these alive? Fundamentalism is lunging at the country every now and then, yet the short-sighted selfish politicians go for feeding on religious sentiments.

The Hindu law courts have gradually diminished the yawning gap between men and women in the society, but in Islamic laws, the rights of women pose a big question. The state that allows its people to frame personal laws on the basis of religious codes can never be termed secular in the true sense of the term. How can I call a nation anti-communal when it patronizes several legal codes on the basis of several religious sects? How can I call it a democracy when it doesn't ensure equal rights of men and women?

Some argue that Indian women have waged a relentless battle against evil practises like the sati, Muslim Personal Law and other forms of gender discrimination. But I have strong reservations on this point. I strongly believe that in India there has never been a true feminist organization or movement as such. Whatever had happened in favour of women was through the generosity of the educated social reformers, who ironically were all men. Women are actually the victims of patriarchal conspiracy that has cast them into the prison called household. Naturally, these women do not know even the 'F' of freedom. They are totally in the dark about their rights. In fact, unless one struggles hard to achieve something, one cannot truly learn to honour it. They, who have acquired certain privileges without their own contribution to any movement, can never realize the significance of the rights. It is hard to involve them in the further struggle for gender justice. Though the women continue to suffer unbearably years after years because of the anti-woman laws; though they are the victims of gang rape; indescribable distress; violent attacks; murders and atrocities of all kinds, very few venture out on the streets in protest. Indian women keep on waiting with their fingers crossed hoping that some magnanimous soul will emerge and lift them from the thorns of life.

As a matter of fact, the culture that hinders the spirit of free-thinking and emancipation, and murders the rights of humans, should never be described as culture. Culture is for the welfare of the mankind. If it harms, either it should undergo overhauling, or it should be cast into the dust bin. Instances are galore in the world history how several cultures gradually became so obsolete that they had to finally embrace inevitable death.

The question before us is how both women's rights and multi-cultural society can coexist? In my opinion, rights must be upheld by any means possible. If culture can keep pace with it, well and good; but if it does not, let it trail behind. The chief and foremost responsibility of women is to uphold their own rights.

***

2

Bengali Men

On the occasion of Sunil Gangopadhyay's birthday, many people have boasted that there were many women in Sunil's life. I wondered whether similarly anyone will boast about many men in a woman writer's life. Would anyone say that this woman wrote many poems for those men and loved many men?

Last time I was in love with any Bengali man was many years ago. In my life in banishment, love had come once or twice. I could never imagine that love could be expressed in a foreign language. But I found that it was possible. After a point of time the mentality of men of East and West becomes similar, both suffer from megalomania. But their behavioural pattern differs vastly. Most of the Bengali men think that one should be in love with seven women at the same point of time. They think that is modernism. They fail to realize that it is neither love nor modernity. It is rather the opposite. These men want to live with a harem like the kings or the landlords of the past. If they cannot do that openly, they want to do it secretly. If that is not possible, they live such a life in their minds. The patriarchal Indian society has given terrible indulgence to men. They have gone so up that from that height the women seem too small, like insects, not like human beings. I was in a society where women are deprived, insulted, tormented, where they are considered only a sex-item. From there, I went to the modern society of the West, where no difference between men and women existed. While living in those countries leading in ensuring equal rights of men and women, I found there a man loves only one woman and spend life with her. They do not go to bed with seven women. If love evaporates, they terminate the relationship. Maybe later, he falls in love with another woman. Then he starts another relationship with that person whom he loves. Marriage papers there are not of much significance. What makes a relationship to continue is love. Not any paper or the bloody eyes of society. In West, if there is want of love, it leads to divorce. But not in this country. That is because the women are helpless, dependent on others; because they are entrusted with the responsibility of raising the children; because they are good commodity to decorate the family with; because they are dressed up slaves of a higher variety.

Relationship continues on the basis of lies, on compromises. In place of love there exists hatred, and still a Bengali man spends a whole life with his wife just because it has become a habit. They feel loving their wives or be satisfied with them is not befitting enough for their manhood. Forget the common men, even the uncommon ones have not learnt to respect women. So they have no regards for women's dignity. I have both friendship and enmity with male authors, poets and artistes. They look like as though they are prepared to sacrifice their lives for their love of women. Probe deeper and you will find each one of them searching for many such women. Faithfulness, which is very important in the West, is irrelevant in the East, in India. But the women must remain faithful. They will not utter the names of their husbands, will call them as 'my husband'. They are like soiled clothes, like stinking inner garments, not usable by another man.

I had sexual relation with only a few Bengali men, and the experience I acquired was horrible. I have also enriched myself with other women's experiences. Western men are conscious about orgasm of their partners, and they first allow the partner to be elevated to the skies and then sail in the sea of his own pleasure. But Bengali men are not bothered about their partners. They clamp the partner with their bodies as though a tiger has got a deer, and complete their eating. Thus, they satisfy the secret desire of raping a woman. Who is there to condemn this brutal exercise of raining semen on a body akin to a pillow and then falling asleep? Most of the Bengali men do not even know that having sex with an unwilling partner is known, in the civilised societies, as rape. And the punishment for it is same for that awarded to any other rapist. Many Bengali men feel they are experts of sex as they have had sexual relationship with many women. But they do not know the details of art or science of women's sexuality; do not know which organ has to be touched to arouse a woman. They do not bother about the satisfaction of the women. Man knows only his pleasure, his joy. Bengali men love themselves nastily. They talk of and write poetry about love, but they do not love women.

In the East, people say that there is free sex in the West. From my long experience, I may claim that I have not witnessed free sex in the West. It is there in West Bengal, in Bangladesh. Here in sexual excitement a man jumps upon any woman. In the West, sex has to be accompanied by love. At least there should be liking for each other. Honesty is also required. It is not that there is no exception. Psychopaths are everywhere. But Bengali psychopaths are not called psychopaths. At times, they are called intellectuals. The problem is that our intellectuals feel they can do anything. Even after crossing 70, they may put their paws on the bosoms of a 17-year-old. And people forgive it as an effort to acquire inspiration for a great creation. The disciples nod. In this country of gurus, anyone becomes a guru if he is taller by two inches. There are disciples all about. They will echo whatever the guru says. I have heard they often present their wives to the guru. The gurus enjoy it to the hilt, and for this regular service provided, they liberally favour their disciples.

Is it so that principles have no role to play in the lives of the Bengali men? Many men have principles. Many others show it outwardly, though inside them they are corrupt. Not all. But the majority I am talking of. They consider their wives as 'domestic wives', as the wives are to be in the house, to take care of the household. At times, they go out with their wives, but that is not an outing with a friend. It is like outing with a mountain on the head. The husband walks ahead of the wife and the latter follows him. This is the mantra of a happy married life. During courtship, the man walks together with his lover. But that is till the time he has not captured her in his palms.

Even the guru of love Rabindranath could not walk with his lover side by side. Then why should we find fault with Ranjan or Ramen? In case of Rabindranath, it was not even a case of one going ahead and being followed, What I have gathered from what I saw and heard, it was like one being at a higher platform and the other at the lower. I am on the chair, you are on the floor next my feet.

There is no tradition of considering one's wife as a friend among the Bengali men. They give a little freedom to their wives and boast of it. As if independence is to be gifted to someone and is not a birthright. It is not only true about the Bengali man. All patriarchal societies are the same. But Bengali man is crazy for the comfort of patriarchy even after being educated, after gaining fame as artists, literary figures and intellectuals.

It is said that the West lacks heart; but the Bengalis fall in love, have hearts, and they can cry. Wrong. I have seen how both men and women cry in the West if a relationship breaks down. They cry crazily. Not for a day or two, for months, years. Seen them to hurt themselves with knives. Seen them to consume poison, to jump on the metro track. They have to go to the psychiatrist with their broken hearts. All around the world, I have seen many great lovers but very few brute lovers like the Bengali men. Rarely seen non-lovers like them.

***

3

Female Body

For so long, it were men who wrote about, sketched and gave shape to the female body with the figment of their mind. Women had no right to write about woman's body. They could write about women's mind, but not about the body. But now women authors and poets are making efforts to break this barrier imposed by men. They write about their bodies in the way they like. If women authors and poets realize that a woman's body is not a man's property, not a monopoly of male authors and poets, then the world of literature would undergo a great transformation.

Bengali society is badly affected by patriarchy. But in Bengali literature, at least some efforts are being made to break the rules and regulations imposed by patriarchy. This is happening perhaps because Bengali women authors and poets are mostly well-educated, self-dependent and conscious about their own rights. But in society at large, women are still helpless, still treated as commodities, exploitable items, still looked down upon as objects of sex.

Women are attending schools and colleges, but are not being educated in proper sense. Women are earning money, but are still dependent on men. Most women are upholders and bearers of the patriarchal system. Women mostly are unaware that they are tortured. In most cases, women are afraid to be liberated from their confinements. This deplorable condition of women is due to the patriarchal system. Women in this society are to serve men. Apparently, she does not have the look of a maidservant, but a closer observation of their mutual relation will reveal it to be so. She is so even when she is his ladylove or his wife. She is a servant of a little higher order. She is to obey the commands and work under the directions of her lover or her husband. A woman has to shape herself the way a man wishes to see her. Her sense of dress, her behaviour, her positive and negative qualities, all are conditioned and given shape by man.

Love is a man's weapon to weaken a woman. There cannot be love between a master and a servant. With a commodity, there can be any emotion attached but love. If a woman expresses her sexual urge, the society severely reprimands her. A woman cannot have sexual instinct; if she has it, she is shameless, fallen, a prostitute. Women will display their body for men, not for themselves. Women will live for men, not for themselves. This is the convention. How many women know the taste of orgasm in sex? There are very few. Most of them think that sex is for men only. Women are to be used by men only for the sake of their pleasure. It is the body of a woman, but the right on it is to be exercised by a man. Women change hands all their lives, from father to lover, from lover to husband, and from husband to son. A woman's life is not her own. She is tied to several males through various relationships. In such a society, when women authors and poets write about their rights on their bodies or their own sexual freedom, that may not reflect the reality; but a form of revolution, however small in scale, and even if theoretical, does take place. These are like sparks, kindled by some, waiting to be spread. Those women who are not writers or poets also have the fire in them, but it hardly finds expression. Therefore, artists and writers always have a significant role in transforming society.

I will not say like the orthodox critics that just writing about the body is not sufficient; it has to qualify the standards of literature. No I would not go for that. In whatever way a woman writes, whatever her subject, if it comes straight from her heart, it is bound to touch others. I do not wish to confine literature within any definition. I feel whatever touches readers' heart, whatever stimulates their mind, that is literature. I think so.

That women are breaking free their shackles is for me perfect poetry. The sound of the chains being rent apart is to me the sweetest music. If anyone writes stories or poems on this subject, that is amazingly beautiful literature, I can say without hesitation. When a woman liberates herself from age-old shackles of convention, even if she cannot write, she is always a poet in my opinion.

***

4

The Beautiful

Anti-aging, exfoliators, masks, eye-brows, eye liners, eye shadow, base makeup, blusher, concealer, illuminators, lip gloss, lip liners, lipstick, nail polish—why thousands of such products are in the market? For whom? We all know, for women. The question is why women should have to use these? Why their real appearance would have to be concealed with so many colours? Why should they make an artificial face? Artificial eyes, and artificial lips? Women use these as they suffer from inferiority complex about their real appearance. Who created this complex? Who decided that a woman's face has many short-comings, and to make it perfect they should use innumerable cosmetics? Only then they would be treated as beautiful!

Women are scared. They won't eat, lest it creates excess fat. Breast should measure this, waist that, abdomen this, hips up to this, thighs this. The vital statistics should match the ideal that has already been decided. So girls have become crazy to fit into that. They are scared of food. Nowadays, as a consequence of not having eaten properly, many of them suffer from Anorexia or Bulimia. But who decided that these measurements of the body of women should be treated as ideal? Who have done so much work on this? Who decided that unless one has such a figure one should not be treated as beautiful, her body not perfect?

The whole world is busy about woman's body. There is no end of variations of their clothes and jewellery. There is almost a war cry. Beautify your body. Use this. Use that. Use different things for your body from head to toe. Keep your body in perfect shape and lustre. But why? And for whom? Won't the girls should once think about it? For whose satisfaction they do all this? Some people emphasize that it is for one's own sake, one's own satisfaction. Is it so? But even the feeling of likings is invoked in the backdrop of long education: can anyone deny that? Who can deny the history of prodding women to go for makeovers?

Women are a commodity in this patriarchal society. Commodity for consumption of men. Whether one agrees or not, this is true. Women should appear exactly the way that arouses the men. So the commodity called women should have such appearance that will make men happy physically and mentally. Whatever the women do in their entire life are all for the sake of men and the patriarchal society. Her chastity, her motherhood, polite character, everything is for serving the men. Men must be able to use women as their property and as slaves. There are various means to capture a woman. The most modern method is called love. Love makes women so much weak, even the strong ones are left without any option other than making them available for all types of use by men. A fiancée undergoes a period of training for appearing in the role of a wife. She passes out with colours if she has enough ability to make sacrifice for him, and if she can forgive all his faults.

Beautiful. This adjective has been made by both men and women. But they all believe in patriarchy. They decide which shape of body be dubbed as beautiful. They control campaigning and marketing for commodities. Campaign works for propagating the view that such and such shapes make a perfect body, and then thousands of things start appearing in the market to fit a woman in that. Treadmill, exercise bike, liposuction, plastic surgery, silicon breasts. Markets are filled with such things and women jump on those. Maybe, they are pushed from behind so that they fall for those. One has to be beautiful. Otherwise, she would have no value; will have no friend; will get no lover; will not be married off in a good family; will not get a good job; she would be forlorn. So, women try their best to be a commodity with a good price at the market. Women do not learn this suddenly one day. A woman is taught all this from her birth. She learns about it from her relatives, from the media, from magazines, particularly from women's magazines. It goes deep in their veins. As a consequence, women acquire much less capability to be conscious of their rights in comparison to men.

The definition of women was different in different country and in different period of time. In the past, plump women were considered beautiful. Now, those are considered as beautiful who are sickly-looking. The sculptures and drawings on women of 19th Century portrayed their heavy lower abdomen in a way as though they all were conceiving. In that age, there was no custom of working out to get rid of excess fat in the abdomen. Now, with the new techniques available, art has also changed. Art has become commercial. All about, the girls are competing with each other to reduce fat. Many people say that in comparison to the girls of this age their grandmothers were much freer. They did not suffer from inferiority complex about their bodies. There was no pressure on them to change their faces. Earlier, any type of slave could do. Now, one needs a beautiful slave. Men are turning more demanding. And, the markets are planning for making women as per demand. The powerful media and the market display samples of beautiful women, and all girls are being trapped. This tremendous pressure to make one beautiful is making their heads blunter. Nixing all their possibilities, they are turning into prostitutes. In the brothel live uncultured prostitutes, outside live cultured prostitutes. Both work for entertaining men.

In this rotten, backward society, physical beauty is the main asset of a woman. Who does not possess that asset lives like a stray dog. Globalization has spread the western definition of beauty everywhere. The whole mankind has internalized it. Chinese women nowadays are craving for big eyes. As though they would change their gene, change the direction of their DNA, if possible. In India, there was never any appreciation for a shaped leg. It came from the West. Now, Indian girls are compelled to expose their legs. The length of trousers and skirts has come up almost to the hips. Broken cheeks have become fashionable. All commodities are being modernized, even the commodity called women. Now it is age of western wind.

I feel scared. Our society is sinking in the depth of sludge of patriarchy. I bristle when I see even the established rational-minded, self-reliant women dressed up like this. Why do they lack in confidence? If it happens with them, what will the common women, who are dependent on others, do? If women are ashamed of their appearance, how will they fight against the age-old shackles of dependence? If without make-up they feel shy, they will further shackle them.

The feminist movement of the West peaked in the 60s. It established the rights of women by giving a tight slap on the face of patriarchy. Men went a step back in those days. But they are now trying to reassert themselves. As a reaction to that feminism, now they want to turn women into toys. It is a conspiracy to push women back by hundred years. Come on girls, shackle yourselves, be beautiful, participate in beauty contests. Sell your flesh. It is a sad thing that feminism did never come to India, but the backlash has come.

Thousands of imageries about different parts of women's body prove that for a woman her body is everything. A boy is either a doctor, or an engineer, or a businessman, or a writer or an artist. A woman is short or tall, dark or fair, beautiful or ugly. A man is known by his work, and a woman by her appearance. Why women acquiesce with men to carry on this difference? Why don't they turn around and say, we will remain as we are.

We are not toys, but human beings of flesh and blood. We believe in originality, not in artificiality. We should be judged by our education, our achievement, our proficiency.

If women were conscious about their rights, they would have understood that they are tormented to the most by this push to be beautiful. Women should spend time, money, everything on this. Men will be in power, whatever their appearance be. No one bothers about their physical appearance. They will be appreciated for their work. There may be exceptions to this, but that is exception. Maybe, in the film-world a man's beauty counts. But that is insignificant. Can there be any plump heroine like Dilip Kumar? If a woman has a body like Govinda, would she get a chance to be a heroine? Amitabh Bachchan is still a megastar with all his wrinkles, but Rekha has to appear without any. Uttam Kumar had roamed about like a hero even when he was aged. Soumitra Chattopadhyay does not have to hide his baldness, fat or the creases of his skin. Their fame as stars has rather increased now. But Suchitra Sen has confined herself in the house. If she appears in the public, her star image will be over. That is why she does not come before the people. She was a great actor, but even she has to earn her fame by her physical beauty. If the skin turns wrinkled, breasts sag, hair turn grey, even a big star loses her esteem. Aparna Sen is far better a director than many men. But without knowing it she has become a victim of patriarchal society. She has to do so much make-up. Look at the world of literature. Would any woman writer survive with such physical features as like Sunil Gangopadhyay or Tarapada Roy?

***

5

I Strain to Listen

I am having some strange experiences in Kolkata. Here girls stepping out of school, college or university—both self-reliant and dependent—go about saying that women have achieved equal rights. If I object, I see sarcasm at the corner of their lips. I translate that sarcasm in my own way. I do not belong to this country, hence I do not know about such matters. Many are struck with amazement if I question them on women's oppression—they have heard something about oppression, but they do not exactly know where or how it happens. If I persist, they sink in thought, and finally, screwing up their nose and lips, declare that if such things happen at all, it is only in villages, certainly not in cities.

I stare at them open-mouthed. I look rather stupid. Perhaps I ask in a very muted tone: Is there no oppression in cities?

They shake their heads. No.

No discrimination?

No. None. Here girls are extremely free.

That's right. Free. Do these girls know what freedom means? I am sure they do not. They think they are free, but it is only because their minds cannot think independently that they say they are free.

Have all rights been achieved?

Yes, all.

Is it really so?

Hmmm... deep in the interior, that is to say in the villages, girls have not achieved so many rights. Poor things, one feels really sorry for them.

As I hear this, I feel even more sorry for the urban girls than those in the villages. The educated girls, who are armed with a college or a university degree and have mingled with a couple or more boyfriends, believe that they have reached the zenith of freedom. She cannot see the shackles on her hands and feet. She does not understand that in this patriarchal society, she is as much a sexual commodity and instrument of child bearing as women were before her. Rather, girls having a brush with modernity enhance man's hunger threefold. These urban, independent women, with vermilion on their head, conch bangles round their hands and their husband's surname to boot, proclaim that they are men's private property. The thing called husband that she has is her security; if this security goes awry, she will be in grave danger and if it falls off, she too will fall off.

What is the purpose of earning money if one does not have the mental strength and courage to stand up alone! I have seen many self-reliant women to calmly submit to rotten, anti-women social customs. It is not possible for even all educated and self-reliant women to have a clear idea about their rights and take every kind of risk to attain those rights.

I have seen many illiterate village women live with greater awareness of their rights than highly educated, urban slave women. A tiny slip on the part of somebody provokes these village women to gird up their loins and hurl abuses not just at him but his entire family. A slight scratch on the body, and they will set professional fighters on the offender. They are experts at extracting their rights. They argue with logic. No girl dares to go to a mosque in the city. But only the other day, women of a village in West Bengal flocked to the mosque to pray. That was indeed revolutionary. Without knowing that women do not really gain anything out of practising religion, they at least did something—something that was forbidden in their society! The path of women is strewn with the litter of a hundred thousand prohibitions. If women have to go forward, their most important duty is to chuck all these prohibitions in the rubbish heap.

It is true that village girls put up a bold resistance from time to time, even make revolutions knowingly and unknowingly, but that does not mean that ignorance and prejudice prevalent in villages is no more existent, and that oppression of women has ceased to exist. All of that is still very much there. Child marriage, dowry system, wife killing, rape and murder stay on happily. However, below the surface, some aspects of the rural scenario have changed considerably. More girls are going to schools than before. Maybe they are being compelled to drop out at a certain stage, but this wave in school-going is new. The mid-day meal system proves that poverty is a major reason for not going to school. Assured of rice, the number of school-goers has risen. If they do not get rice, they resort to other means to procure rice. A, B, C, D cannot drive out hunger. Reasons for girls dropping out of schools include household chores and early marriages. It is seen that those who do not have to face these problems easily finish school and go on to college. Cycling from one village to another, they go lighting up the village roads. How many city girls ride bicycles? I have not seen a single girl cycling in Kolkata till date.

Since there are more villages than cities, since there are more village girls than city girls, women's education needs to be really stepped up in the villages. For years, a fraud has been perpetuated by marking off those who can barely sign their names as educated. Let this stop now. The word 'educated' does not mean just being able to sign one's name; it also does not mean acquiring a degree by mugging up history and geography. To be educated means to be educated about your rights. The greatest education is to be aware of the fact that a woman is nobody's toy, no doll, no servant, no object and no tool.

The progress of a society depends on the progress of women in that society. This is what I believe in. Women make up half of the total population. If half the population remains uneducated and dependent, if they remain persecuted and oppressed, if the talent, intelligence, strength and power of this huge section are of no use to the society, then that society is bound to remain backward. If women lag behind, progress too lags behind. If women lag behind, civilization lags behind.

India's economic development is undoubtedly reaching for the sky. However, the overall development of women in comparison is almost plumbing the depths of the ground. There is no strong women's movement in the country that can fight for a uniform civil code and healthy life free from the grip of religion and prejudices and, thereby, ensure women's rights, human rights and equal rights. Then what will that economic development be like when half of the population would remain deprived of their own rights! Such development is not a real development, not a development which one can be proud of. Both Saudi Arabia and Sweden are rich countries. But the difference between the two is appalling. If Sweden scores 100 in democracy, freedom of speech and human rights, Saudi Arabia will score a zero. One is civilized, the other undoubtedly uncivilized.

No one is ever going to gift liberty to women. Women have to fight and win liberty for themselves. Women themselves do not know from what they are being deprived of and how. For centuries, it has been drilled into women that they are a breed of slaves. How will women achieve liberty! Nevertheless, I strain to listen. I strain to listen to the sound of women rising from a long, long sleep.

***

6

I Am Proud to Be Wilful

The rain has come in torrents, accompanied by loud bursts of thunder. I set out from my house. I wish to be drenched in the rain.

Why do you want to get wet?

I feel like it.

Feel like it?

Yes, feel like it.

What will people think about it!

What will they think?

They will think you have gone crazy.

Let them think so.

You'll fall sick if you get wet in the rain!

What sickness?

You'll catch flu.

Doesn't matter.

All this doesn't suit your age.

Which age does it suit?

It would have been fine if you were 16 or 17.

Many would have had problems with that too. Anyway, who has made this list that specifies what should be done at a certain age and what shouldn't be done?

Society.

Do we exist for society or does society exist for us? It is human beings who make the rules. Again, it is human beings who break the rules. No rule lives on for an indefinite period of time.

Our conversation went on and on before finally coming to an end with the word 'wilful'. If the word 'wilful' means 'determined to act according to one's wishes', then I certainly am wilful. One hundred per cent so. It is my life. I shall decide what to do and what not to do. Why should anybody else decide for me? Each person's life belongs to that person. Every person should know what she or he wants to do with it. I do not consider a person who does not have a will of her or his own to be an adult. I do not consider a person who does not act according to her or his wish, or is afraid to do so, to be sane.

Now the question may arise, what if somebody wishes to murder someone else? What if somebody wishes to rape someone? My personal opinion is that I do not believe in that sort of wilfulness that causes harm to the others. Now, 'harm' too has different meanings. What if somebody says, 'You cannot condemn my religion because your censure hurts my religious sentiments?'

If to hurt someone physically means to cause that person harm, then why not hurting someone's sentiment will amount to causing harm! In this case, my opinion is that the human mind is often a den of superstitions and ignorance and we should try to rid the mind of that. It is the responsibility of the conscious people to take initiative in this. Here another question may arise, what makes me consider myself, and not a fundamentalist, to be a conscious person? I have a hundred reasons for not considering a fundamentalist to be a conscious person. The fundamentalist too is free to put forth his own arguments. But with the power of reasoning I possess and the values I have developed, I can refute the arguments of a fundamentalist as unscientific and illogical and remain firm in my opinion. I consciously never hurt anyone physically. I never do something that causes financial loss for any honest person. I do not repent my wilfulness. I have never had to repent till date. I have broken many a social taboos. People have labelled it as wilfulness; I have called it freedom. My conscience is clear. Whatever I do, from my point of view, does not tantamount to injustice done to anyone. To be honest to one's own self, to be irreproachable to one's own self, is worth a lot.

When I was a teenager, prohibitions barred every step. You will not step out of doors. You will not play. You will not go to the movies or theatres. You will not go to the terrace. You will not climb trees. You will not look at any boy. You will not have an affair. But I did everything. I did all those because I wished to do those. It is not that I wished to do those because I was forbidden to do them. My father forbade me to do a lot of other things. For example, he told me never to get into a pond; I did not, because I could not swim. I was afraid that if I got into the pond, I would not enjoy it, rather I could get drowned if I was careless. My father told me not to climb the railings on the terrace. I never climbed them, because I felt the railings were too slender and it would be disastrous if I slipped and fell off. When I am about to do something, I do not consider what others have to say about it; rather, I judge it myself, reflecting on the arguments I myself render. I confront my desire with great honesty. It is not easy for girls, whose wishes are never given the slightest value by this patriarchal society, to give shape to their desires. But I never saw any reason why they should not be given shape. I know I can never bear to see myself as a cowardly, defeated figure, head bowed and knees bent in humble submission.

My struggle is for the truth, for equality, for beauty. I have to be wilful if I have to carry on this struggle. This struggle is impossible if one is not wilful. If I have to hold my head high even in private life, I have to be wilful. If I act according to the wishes of someone else, I shall become dependent on others. If I act on the advice of others, if I am guided by the ideas of others, then I am mentally retarded. If I have to lead my life on the mercy doled out by others, then I am certainly not self-reliant. There the joy of wilfulness is absent. There is no freedom of thought, no freedom of intellect; it is just like being driven like a machine. The very thought suffocates me. It is better to be dead than live such an insufferable life.

Men have always acted wilfully. Society is under their control. Wilfulness is necessary for women. Woman has to put her desires under lock and key, and by doing so, pose as a so-called good girl in this society—a well-behaved girl, a sensible girl, a polite girl, a modest girl. It is time she took out the key from under her apron. It is time she opened the lock and released her desires, like the birds, into the sky. Let women become wilful everywhere.

Otherwise, they will not comprehend what freedom means. Otherwise, they cannot perceive the beauty of life.

I know what freedom means. I feel the importance of freedom at every moment. Whether I am alone, or part of a twosome, or in a surging crowd, I never donate my freedom, or lose it anywhere. I write about freedom and rights and I believe in what I write. I live what I believe in. I am a mentally strong, economically self-reliant and morally independent person. Men cannot tolerate this. Men do not like such power in a woman. They want to have woman in the palm of their hand, so that they can crush her beneath their feet. If woman does not allow herself to be crushed, she is not a good woman. If she does not allow herself to be crushed, she is a fallen woman. If she does not allow herself to be crushed, she is wilful. Many people think that to be wilful is to be ready to jump into bed with any man at any time, to have sexual relationships. But wilfulness does not mean anything of the kind. I think to be wilful is not to sleep with men. The general rule is that a woman has to sleep with a man. If a man calls, she has to drop whatever she is doing and rush to him. If a woman does not sleep with a man, if she does not feel like it, then that woman is definitely wilful. Why should men like such wilful women! The woman who does not give herself up to a man's pleasure, does not give herself up for the satisfaction of a man's physical and mental lust, for the satisfaction of his wantonness and perversion—men not only label her as wilful but also insult by calling her a prostitute.

I do whatever I please. I do not do anything by destroying anybody. Because I am wilful, I can well comprehend the meaning and worth of life. If I had not been wilful, if I had sacrificed myself at the altar of the wishes of others, I would never have understood who I am or why do I exist! If a person fails to recognize his or her own self, who will she or he recognize then! If I had not been wilful, then, perhaps, I could not have written a single sentence of this article.

***

7

The Past and Present
of Bengali Women

Majority of the Bengali Hindus, even those who have passed out from college or university, who have sharp knowledge of politics and economics, believe that Bengali means only Bengali Hindus. They do not know that Bengali Muslims, Buddhists, Christians and atheists are also Bengalis. This ignorance of Bengali Hindus is getting fearsome dimension day-by-day. People of East Bengal or Bangladesh are generally called Bangladeshis. There can be Bangladeshi cows, Bangladeshi laws, but how human beings can be Bangladeshis? Bengali race did not come into being the day Bangladesh was formed. Bengalis are still Bengalis with their age-old language and culture, only the name of the country is changing again and again for political reasons. Why should the onus of that come on the race? Those religionists who wanted to finish off rich and secular Bengali culture and replace that with Islamic culture to destroy the country, they have changed the constitution to replace Bengali nationalism with Bangladeshi nationalism. They have replaced secularism with Islam as state religion with the same intention.

Bengali Muslims are more in number than Bengali Hindus, so it is likely that ultimately the culture of Bengali Muslims will be treated as Bengali culture. It must be mentioned here that the culture of Bengali Muslims is different from that of non-Bengali Muslims. And it is also different from Bengali Hindu culture despite many similarities. For historical reasons, the language and culture of Bengali Muslims is richer as it came under influence of different foreign cultures and languages.

Bengali women may have faith in any religion—Hinduism, Buddhism, Christianity or Islam, or they may be atheist. Whenever I ask myself how are the Bengali women in Bengal, how are they spending their day and night, I feel pained. In a society dominated by religion, women cannot live with the rights of a human being. When religion dominates, patriarchy also dictates terms. Where religion and patriarchy are held in high esteem, women there turn into slaves or sexual commodities or machines for producing children. Some people talk of change. The villages are turning into tiny towns, tiny towns into bigger ones and bigger towns are becoming cities. The cities have big houses, schools, colleges and universities. Those Bengali women, who were debarred from stepping out or from educating themselves, are now passing out from schools and colleges, studying in universities, taking up jobs and earning money. In the cities, it seems the change has gone sky-high. But how many women have enjoyed its fruit? Eighty per cent of women still cannot read and write. Among those people living below poverty line, the majority are women. The women are suffering. Not only patriarchy is lashing them, poverty is also bleeding them. But are the middle class or upper class women living happily? No. Women have no class, no caste. Whichever class they belong to, whichever caste, they are oppressed. The mode of oppression varies, but essentially it is the same.

Are those who are educated exercising their rights? Are they independent? Women are, whether educated or illiterate, oppressed. This is because religion, patriarchy, culture and society are against women. The women without education cannot learn the rules and regulations of patriarchy as accurately as the educated. Educated women are being directed by their husbands. She cannot go for employment unless her husband permits it. Those who are employed, they have turned economically independent, but not self-reliant. A rotten culture still keeps the women under the men.

If culture goes against humanity, becomes a stumbling block on the road of equality, why should we nurture it? We must rather destroy it. If the culture turns into a closed water body instead of a flowing river, why should we swim in it? Till the culture of the Bengalis are reformed and made unbiased, there is nothing to be proud about it. Particularly, for the women.

To prove it as civilized, the country has abolished some anti-women customs. But the mentality of majority of the men and women are still fearsomely patriarchal. To make the women conscious of their rights, what is urgently needed is changing the master-slave relationship between the men and women. From childhood, one should be taught about equal rights of men and women. Equally important for the children, is to see the equal rights being practised by men and women. People learn more from their experience than from what they have studied.

If women's condition were really better, then things like choosing the bride or paying dowry would not have been there. There would have been no female foeticide. Some say women are oppressed in the villages, not in the cities. In West Bengal, most cases of female foeticide take place in Kolkata. Terrible brothels are smirking in front of everybody's eyes. Men crowd there to insult the women, to annihilate women's prestige, to trample under feet her rights. Trafficking, killing, rape or mass-rape of women no longer shocks people. These things happen more in the cities than in the villages.

The image of Bengali woman ingrained in the minds of people is a woman wearing a sari. If aged, then worn plainly with a ring of keys tied at one corner of the border. If young, colourful saris worn with pleats. If Hindu, a dot on forehead and vermilion in the parting. Bangles and earrings should be there; nose-pins may or may not be. Men have dictated how should be the Bengali women. Polite, loving and shy. Independent, wilful women do not match with the image of Bengal women. She should devote herself to household work. In between, should sing with string-instruments or harmonium. Half-lying on the mat, should write poetry or gossip in the early afternoon. Should wait eagerly at the door for her husband and should serve him food cooked by her. Her own things should come at the end. She should pray for all creatures of the world, should tolerate all atrocities, should serve everybody and be pious—this is Bengali woman. Bengali women mean Suchitra Sen, Shabana, Jamini Roy, Kamrul Hassan.

This image is an imposed one. Many women have broken out of this. They do whatever they want; wear whatever they like. They break the barriers, wear western outfits, are fashionable in their language, have waves in their bodies. But even they do not cross certain limit. An invisible string controls them. They go for marriage, serve their husbands, produce children, devote their lives and tolerate everything. They look modern, but they are not so. They start with promises of new things, but ultimately go round the same circle as like their grandmothers. It happens to them for they do not understand the meaning of modernism.

Those who are oppressed for not having male sex-organ; who are deprived of their rights and live a poor, dependent life being burden on the others; those who have no security in family or society, how does it matter what caste, society or country do they belong to! Bengali men can be proud of Bengal. For women, it does not matter.

Bengali men fulfil their interest on the foundation of sacrifices made by the women. Women get nothing. Their lives remain blank. Even the husband or the family does not return her dues. Earlier, the babus used to go to the Baiji's. Now they go for many other women after insulting or ignoring their wives. This is an exhibition of brute force. According to scriptures, they had the right of polygamy, and they practised that. Now Hindus cannot marry more than once, but the Muslims can. They enjoy four wives and torture women mentally and physically. The men feel that it is legitimate for them to have sex with many women. But, women can have many men only by turning into prostitutes. A Bengali woman cannot talk of sex, cannot divorce even if the man is impotent, cannot demand share of property and cannot do anything for her own happiness. Everything is prohibited. Anger, breaking things, tearing up, everything.

Those who still break the rules, who demand, who speak of their rights and snatch them, those who do not look back, challenge inequality, do not care for what people say, do something new, they are the women who have come out of the traditional pattern of suffocating lives of Bengali women. They are making new image of the Bengali woman by tearing up the old image of women with heads covered, vermilion on their parting, property of the males. They are very few in number. If they save the women from exploitation, make them conscious, then all women should say: "Though we have social relation with the men, our identity is not of being mother, sister, daughter, aunt or grandmother of men, we are different, not property of men or patriarchy, we are human beings. We live with the rights of human beings, we trample under feet religion, culture, customs, laws, whatever stand as impediments to our liberty." Only then Bengali women shall be able to break the image of dedication to become real human beings. The new definition of Bengali women shall be: protesting, intelligent, believers in equality, strong, conscious, bold, determined, arrogant. Only then I will be proud of the Bengalis.

***

8

My Lovers

In my adolescence, the word love was a forbidden one. As I stepped into the age of courtship, I noticed how tecnage boys and young men started casting flirtatious glances at me; I too felt tempted to reciprocate, but for me love was a taboo. Whatever else I do, I should not fall in love. Ironically, all the movies and theatres I saw had in them a story of love. The novels or short stories I read, was all about love. The songs I listened to were love songs! Love was everywhere; but it should not enter my life. The more love-less life one had, the better. This was the kind of environment in which I grew up. Since love was a forbidden thing, the curiosity was stronger. My father beat me several times for I was in love. He would lash me, confine me, stop my meals and debar me from my school and college, though he believed that studies are the only thing on which the students should concentrate.

During adolescence, I admired a couple of boys. This adoration was limited to distant glances and 'I love you' slips. I learnt the art of courtship from my *chhotda* (brother). He was senior to me by eight years. He was having an affair with a girl who lived in the same neighbourhood. I used to secretly read *chhotda's* letters written to her. During his absence, I would open the tin suitcase to read the love letters hidden under an old newspaper used as a mat of the suitcase. *chhotda* used to pass the letters on the sly to the girl through her window. Later, he wooed another girl to whom he wrote similar *billet-doux*. In all these letters addressed either to Dolly Pal or Gita Mitra, he wrote how deeply he was in love with her. Reading those letters, I learnt what love was, what it meant by a heartthrob or a sleepless night. In those days, I also read secretly an adult magazine entitled *Kamana* (lust) which I found hidden under the bed of my *barda* (elder brother) and that was the source of my first lesson in sex.

I started writing at an early age when I was a teenager. In those days, the news magazines and tabloids dishing out stories on art, cinema and literature sold like hot cakes. Pen-friendship was in great demand through those magazines. Whenever I wrote something, I was flooded with letters inviting me to be pen-friends. All from young and attractive men. Some used to send photographs also. I would reply back to the guys whose photographs or handwriting or language I liked. Some would become friends soon, and some would turn into over-protective elder brothers showering rains of advice. From writing letters to pen-friends of distant cities, I turned to writing love letters. My maiden letter was to a poet. I myself was then the editor and publisher of a poetry magazine at the age of 17. The poet had offered his love, so I must reciprocate—the equation was like this. My mind was filled with *chhotda's* love letters hidden in the tin box, his whistles and glances at the girl standing at her window in the evenings. I had not seen the poet, nor did I know how old he was, where he lived, what his academic qualifications were; he just asked for my 'life' and without a second thought I replied: "Only this much! Here it is."

After I swam across the seven seas of love, I met him. No, I could not look straight into his eyes. After pronouncing a couple of sentences in passive, I ran home. I could not admire his appearance—his height, breath and the bearded face. Nevertheless, I was obsessed with the concept of 'love'. A first year medical student, I was then slim and pretty. I was a staunch admirer of his poetry and infatuated with 'love'. His appearance became subservient to his poetic talents and love. I was like a touch-me-not creeper who could not look at his eyes. It took as many as five years for me to be intimate with him in talks. I slept with him some years after marrying him. We had tied the nuptial knot in secret, before the notary public. Nobody in my home had the inkling of it. I had kept it a secret as I knew if my father got wind of it, he would kill me. I was a medical student and my lover was a vagabond, a hobo. We were living in two different towns. I burnt midnight oil to write letters to him. He too wrote regularly. I would read each of his letters again and again. They were not letters, they were poems! The letters were wrapped in yellow covers. As I would lay my hand on them, a queer sensation would run through my heart. I cannot explain even today how it was. Before opening a letter, I would keep it on my palm for long. Something inexplicable arose from the letters and cooled me. I felt like hearing the sound of rain, as though a shower has started. Then one day, the countdown ended. One fine morning, leaving my friends and relations in tears, I eloped with him. Just like my *chhotda* who had once left home with Gita Mitra. In courtship, I followed *chhotda* in every step. The seeds of intense love hidden in those letters inside the tin box grew up into a large sprawling tree and secured *chhotda* first, then me. So tightly it gripped me that I could not make out that my lover actually did not love me. He was a philanderer, rather a womanizer, and of course proved unfaithful to me. To him there was no basic difference between his wife's body and that of a prostitute. He just wanted a formal wife, her care and free sex every night. He was a carrier of venereal diseases that he did not hesitate to infect me with. No, he was not at all a lover, he was just a male person. He was like any other man, while I was merely a deaf and dumb, silly lass, madly in love with him.

Next, love visited me occasionally like gentle afternoon breeze that carried the touch of life. Someone looked at me with appreciation in his eyes, someone walked with me holding my hand, someone whispered a song into my ears. Then there was a long pause of solitude during my turbulent youth. This lonely life enhanced my confidence and self-respect hundred times more than before. It made me strong-willed, haughty. A self-reliant physician living alone! Not only that, I was writing fiery articles on women's liberty. The country was going berserk by those writings.

On one such crossroads of life, the door of my heart opened by a sudden gust of spring wind. I bumped into an exceptionally handsome youth. I had a crush on him. His tall and handsome figure, hair, eyes, nose, lips and chin enthralled me. I glanced at him copiously. One day, I was gawking at him so desperately that in embarrassment he removed his eyes from me. My eyes stood still on his face. The hundred arrows from the quiver of my admiration must have struck him. One day, I drank a cocktail of orange juice and some drops of vodka that made me blind drunk. As my steps staggered, he stretched out his hand for me. The touch made me more intoxicated. Each part of my body longed to be with his. That was the beginning of a strong, arduous, indomitable romance. For the first time in my life, I developed relation with a married man. I had no other option but to love him. We roamed about the city, walking side by side with hands clasped together. We went to parties together, and while the house was filled with friends and relatives, we slipped into a vacant room.

Yes, I passionately loved the man and I shall be involved with him. I would allow none to interfere with my freedom. No, none. Never before had I enjoyed my freedom so intensely as then. In comparison to my beauty, my joy of freedom, my human feelings, my liveliness, my youth, he appeared to be much blurred, faded. I simultaneously ran an affair with him and lived separately—an experience that gave me immense peace. My lover had no free access to my day-to-day life, to my literary career, to my private premises, to my aesthetic desires; yet, in moments of romantic arousal, I felt free to kiss him, to make him lie down on the bed and keep fondling all over his body. With him, I floated by the stream, soaked and drenched and lost in tumultuous storm. I had transformed him into my lover not through sacrifice but by passion. He could no more imagine a life without me. I was the only dear and near one in his life. That was a time when people were uniting against my writings, gathering against my ideology and my struggle for equality. Fundamentalists and male chauvinists were demanding to send me to gallows; they were baying for my blood!

One day, I found myself running for life. Wrapped up in the blanket of darkness, I looked around for my lover. Where was he? There was no trace of him. Instead, he was spending his secured married life, keeping a safe distance from me. My faith crumbled down like a nine-storey building that was razed to the ground by a devastating earthquake.

Afterwards, I was banished to a chilling life in North Europe. Pangs of solitude constantly pricked me. Years passed by in melancholy. I was on constant move, from one country to another. In the whirlpool of fame and acclamation, I was gasping for breath. My heart was drought-stricken and body covered with moss. That very mossy body trembled again by the touch of another man on a quiet, lonely, unbearable night. After a little intimacy, I started living together with him. Gradually, I began to feel that I did not want a man, I wanted a lover. He was a French youth, younger to me by six years. I was in my late 30s, living in Paris, the city of love. He visited me on holidays from Tuluz. Sitting on the river bank, we kissed and our kisses must have cast a soothing effect on the river Sein. We kissed in the bus, in the car, in the boat, in the plane, in public places and everywhere. We were so engrossed in what we were doing that we were oblivious of others' presence around us. No, we did not want to sport our love to anyone. Perhaps, this is called love that compulsively obsesses the mind. My French lover proved that my lessons on love from the Bengali lover were not flawless. The way my French lover touched me, the way he admired me, it cast a spell over me. No, I had not known before that love could be really of so much beauty, equality and glory. His kisses, his embrace, his foreplays took me to a new world of love, where no Bengali male had dreamt of taking me ever before. I had never known before that sex could be so great an art.

Breaking my solitude like a glass, the French lover had offered me a sky. He had taught me real love. But the difficulty was that he longed to possess me. He wanted me to live with him. He was passionately in love with me. He said he would kill himself if he failed to get me. His life would turn out meaningless without me. But I made it clear that it will not be possible for me to leave Paris for Tuluz to live with him. I proposed him to come to Paris or else live separately. He would not agree. He felt like being belittled. He accused me of making him a toy-boy. He wept violently saying: "You're famous; why should you bother to love a trifle like me?" But does love distinguish between a big shot and a small fry? But who cares my words? He weeps for me but a little later gnashes his teeth and abuses me "You swine!" If women do not oblige men, they can even tear and snap them into pieces. Man enjoys not so much in loving a woman as he loves in controlling her. On one hand, his jealousy and inferiority complex and on the other, my determination sent us on the brink of separation. For the sake of love, I could not sacrifice my life. The vast stretch of life was before me and so I could not confine myself into a prison for sheer fun! Never.

Leaving their expertise in love, passion and sexuality, the men of the West or East carry the same attitude towards women: both of them look upon women as inferior to men. Why should I compromise with this myth?

After this, I passed a quiet life for a couple of years. A life without any man. I was absorbed in friendship, travelling and studies, in philosophy and art. At one point of time, I started visiting Bengal. My favourite city and favourite people. My heart was filled with love. As the door of my heart was left open, a Bengali man stormed into it. It was like adolescent romance—without touch or sleeping with him. I was then a research scholar in Harvard University. I could not concentrate on my work. My heart was Bengali and dream was a Bengali. He was senior to me by 20 years, yet I soon made him so intimate as though he belonged to my peer group! Love wafted through e-mails, telephones—daily from Cambridge to Kolkata and from Kolkata to Cambridge. Good morning and good night—each day and night. Love in poetry; love in every word and line. I was being drifted out by the mad rush of love.

I remember that day—the day we were going to meet each other. I was trembling in excitement at the prospect of his embrace. In the name of kiss, he bit my lips, in the name of love, he scratched my breasts. Then pinching my cheek, he departed. His love was limited to that. I was bowled over. My French lover would fondle me by his feathery touch all over my body. But what sort of fondling was it by the Bengali lover? But only this savagery is expected from a man hailing from a society that looks upon woman as nothing more than a sex commodity. Nevertheless, I failed to contain my passion for him. I longed for his company. No, he was not there to indulge himself in a day-and-night courtship. He would drop in for a few minutes in the evenings. This is supposed to be the practice in this city for those involved in extra-marital relationship. I, who took love so seriously, was really hurt at this bizarre interpretation of legitimacy and illegitimacy in love. But, what surprised me most was that while drowning me neck deep in love, my lover never hesitated to commit the unpardonable crime of suppressing the fact that he was impotent.

He remained a friend. But I was then about 40, and my body longed for company. Perhaps, it surpassed my thirst when I was in my 30s and even 20s. Once again I was borne aloft by and drenched through and through by another strong gale of love. I met a poet. Crushing the prevailing customs of the conservative society, I hung around with the poet. He was my morning, my afternoon, my evening, my night. I taught him the art of love; I gave him lessons on 32 methods of erotic art. And then I found he bore all over his body the scars of sexually-transmitted diseases.

My world reeled like a spindle. Someone gives the blows of hammer on me to make me steel. But in vain! The poet gave me pleasure all right, but provided pain three times more. I did not weep as I had done in my earlier life. No, the poet did not know what love is. He was too heartless to look back at my pain. I was bleeding so much that when one winter night a man laid his warm hand on my hand, pat I turned into a river. In the darkness that touch carried me away. I realized I was in love again. Like an innocent child, this peculiar man longed to bind me in platonic love. But why he wanted this or what he exactly wanted I did not understand. Why should I walk with him in dense fog when I have vowed to remove the clouds and invite sunshine?

I have given generously to males. No matter whether he was a true lover, or a cheat, I unfolded my whole heart to him. At times, in the dead of night, when the breeze sportingly sweeps over me, I feel lonely, awfully lonely. I have a life of a busy writing career that brings me in touch with millions of people. The other life I have is absolutely personal. From the very beginning, I am a loner in this world. Quite now and then, someone, like a flash of light, breaks my loneliness and then disappears quietly. I call only a handful of men as my 'lovers,' but as I get back to my senses, it is not that I do not say to myself, "None of them is worth being my lover." The lovers craved my company for obvious reasons, but no one desired me for he loved me. Someone wanted me for my name, someone for wealth, someone for fame, someone for my body and someone for heart. All were terribly demanding. But my own likings were ignored.

They are all cheats, hypocrites, cowards. Was anyone of them a real lover? Today in the afternoon of my youth, I realize that I used to be happy in those days mistaking the sad days for days of happiness. I overturned my heart to love them; but I have realized that they were all males, just males but none of them was a lover.

***

9

A Room of my Own

Virginia Woolf wrote a very important book, *A Room of One's Own*. The year was 1929. Women lived in many different houses—father's house, husband's house, brother's house, uncle's house, son's house. Women had no house of their own and they had to live in somebody else's house. Since women had no money, they could not live life according to their inclination; they had no privacy. It was Virginia Woolf who so long ago said that a woman badly needed a room of her very own, a room where she would not be bothered by anybody or where nobody would interfere. Today women in the West are getting the opportunity and environment to live alone. Women there are much more self-reliant than they ever were; the spectre of prejudice does not haunt society as much as before. But things are really miserable for women in the East.

The millstone of patriarchy, religion and a thousand prejudices still hang heavily around her neck. Social reformers have arranged for education and even self-reliance of girls; but has that changed things at all? How many women have a room or a house of their own and live completely alone, leading lives according to their own wishes? How many women have their own income, their own houses? How many women fly about where they wish and do exactly as they feel? How many women enjoy their own freedom, their own wilfulness? The few who try to live such lives are showered with suggestions and advices from hordes of men night and day. Hence, women cannot really relish the joy of living alone.

I am living alone for years now. But it is not that circumstances forced me to live alone. I used to dream of living alone. And I realized the dream. For this, I had had to face more than my share of storms and stress. After deciding that I would stay alone, that I would not live with any man, I scoured the city for a house I might rent. But could I get a house! All landlords sent me off with a flea in my ear. First, they were shocked to see me. What? A miserable woman has come to rent a house? I am a doctor. I have worked in big hospitals in the city. Even after knowing that I was well able to pay the rent, nobody would let out their house to me because I had no male guardian. No father, no brother, no husband. After a lot more wandering about and a lot of effort, I found a house. I had to beg and plead with the landlord to allow me to stay without a man. Finally, the landlord relented grudgingly. But he insisted that though I did not need to have a man with me, I could not live alone. I would have to have somebody live with me. Somebody would have to live with me because I am a woman. A woman is only a body, a body that which induces greed. Women are nothing but bodies. Men will covet such a body. Without a male to keep vigil over her, a girl will lose her virginity in no time, her chastity will go for a toss. Filthy flies will sit on the half-eaten pineapple lying on the veranda. Who in the wide world wants to deal with a single woman! One winces in shame and fear when one hears of a single woman. Girls are not supposed to stay alone. Respectable girls do not live alone. Girls of disrepute do, prostitutes do. I am a busy doctor associated with a renowned hospital. But, because I live alone, my neighbours give me the kind of dirty looks and fiendish smiles that they usually reserve for prostitutes.

I brought my mother to my house. One woman is the same as two women. I could not live in that house for long. The sneering disdain of the neighbours made my landlord throw me out one day. No one gives shelter to a single woman; even one's best friend steers clear. I had to live in hotels for months. I managed only because I was firm that I would live alone. I was so resolute then that I could have crossed an impenetrable forest even on a pitch-black night. I could have swum across a frozen sea. The barbaric rules of society often tried to shatter me into pieces, wring me out of my shape and drain me to exhaustion. But I remained firm. I have understood with my life how risky it is for a girl to ignore all men and stay alone in this horrendously woman-hating society.

After suffering further in this manner, after being hit and bruised, I was forced to buy an apartment in a respectable neighbourhood. I thought I would no longer have to be a victim of harassment, derision and ridicule. But problems cropped up even in the house I had bought for myself. It all began when I started having an affair with a young man. Who is this youth? What relationship do you share with him? He is my lover, I replied. The word 'lover' was like a bombshell. Nobody could bear the fact that I was going around with him, that my lover sometimes spent the night at my house. Since I lived alone, my neighbours kept an extra sharp eye on me. No, I have never cowered before ridicule, slogans, orders or protests. I have always unhesitatingly done what I felt to be right. I Kept my spine straight and taut and held my head high. Nobody feeds me or clothes me. So, how does it matter to anybody who I go to bed with?

Though I have not seen too many men, I have seen quite enough. Isn't one quite enough! Since I did not think one to be enough, I wanted to amuse myself with another. I found both to be made of the same stuff. Love and longing for a handful of days. Made for each other. Cannot live without you, will die for you... and so on. And then back to square one. His father and grandfather emerge from behind the mask of the lover and he shows his true colours. Before living together, he believes in equal rights of men and women two thousand per cent, he is the *numero uno* champion of women's emancipation. But as soon as the couple begins to live together, he will lie down cosily and order her about, demanding tiger's milk and giraffe's head. She has to get hold of everything, because he is a man, he has a three or four-inch long thing between his thighs. He wants a whole lot of things for himself and does not want a lot of things for me. He does not want that I should talk to any man other than him for quite a while, he does not want that I should go anywhere without his permission. He wants to lead a wonderful life after having me in his fists. He fails to understand that I feel suffocated in his clammy palms. He fails to understand this because of that three or four-inch long thing of his. That puny thing is quite enough to blunt a man's senses to an awful extent.

As long as my brain continues to function, I shall live alone. Does any girl live with a man unless she is stark, staring mad! Does anyone consciously wish to be a man's doll! Actually, that is just how girls are brought up right from birth. I too was brought up that way. But at a certain point of time I resisted. No, I will not be a doll; I will not be a commodity. Then what will I be? I will be a human being. I will be 'I'. My entire person is steeped in this resolution. Since I do not let any man stay with me in my house, it does not follow that I do not wish to fall in love with a man. I cannot live without love for a moment. As I am a heterosexual, I cannot stem the tremendous attraction I feel for a handsome man. And if the hunk possesses extraordinary learning, intellect, talent and a sense of humour to boot, if he has a big heart, I cannot but fall in love with him. When I fall in love, it is for all 24 hours of the day. Men today think of love as a one or two-hour fling. By love they mean stepping outside the house to grab a girl, bite her lips, scratch her breasts and ejaculate all over her, all the while keeping the wife back home in absolute darkness. This is not my idea of love. By love I understand tremendous passion. I want my lover to be my best friend, someone with whom I can readily share everything that happens throughout the day and night, all the joys and sorrows of life. Someone who is not a liar, a cheat, a swindler or a lumpen. Someone for whom I am ever thirsty. Someone who makes me forget the world, someone in whom I find my world. Someone who remains with me, by me. Someone with whom I am forever flying in the sky, astir with the joy of an orgasm.

I want him to stay by me does not mean that he has to share my bed every night, or that we have to live under the same roof.

If he is in my heart, he can be miles away and yet remain in my heart. I will make love to him when I wish to. In my house, or his, or anywhere else. But he has to get out of my house by midnight. It is not that I shall insultingly throw him out. I shall show him the door lovingly, showering him with kisses. He may spend the night in my house occasionally, but as my guest, not as a member of my house. This is my decision. I shall not live together with my lover till the last drop of patriarchy congealed in his head is eliminated. I do not believe in marriage. For a long time, I did believe in living together, but not anymore, for living together soon reveals the real self of a man to such a monstrous extent that he begins to think of himself as a husband, and he starts to behave in exactly the same way in which husbands inflict physical and mental torture on women. In this utterly patriarchal society, I deeply believe in living separately rather than living together. My principle is the same for men in the West. Outwardly, there may be some superficial differences between men of the East and the West, but man is basically the same everywhere. The ingredients are all the same.

I am well-acquainted with the joys of living alone. Living alone boosts one's self-confidence. One comes to respect oneself more. Living alone enhances one's mental strength; one has a deeper understanding about who and what one is. Living alone means one does not have to shoulder the servile responsibility of keeping someone else happy and satisfied. One can comprehend the real meaning of freedom. Living alone means one can live life to the lees. A human being has only one life, and after all is said and done, after all the sounds die out, every human being is essentially alone.

***

10

Savagery to Common Civil Code

Muslim militants commit incredible and shocking acts at regular intervals. Bombing diverse targets and creating panic are common incidents. People watch all these in bewilderment. But, irrespective of religion, any terrorist group can perpetrate these crimes. However, at regular intervals, they play such games with women that perplex the Indian people. It appears they have assumed sole responsibility for carrying out such deeds. It is not that such tricks are not played with non-Muslim women or that they enjoy absolute liberty. That is not the reality.

Everywhere in India, women are more or less in shackles of servitude. However, while the savagery on Hindu women has its limits, limitless acts of savagery are perpetrated against the Muslim women. The Muslim males make it more explicit than the others that women exist only as an instrument of satisfying sexual urge of the males, as bonded slaves and as objects of pleasure of the masculine gender. A father-in-law has raped his daughter-in-law. Whether or not they have symbols of Islam or circumcision in their genital, all men ravish women physically and in their minds. But, how is it that a woman would be compelled to accept the rapist as her husband? Even the most uncivilized people never issued such a fatwa. Of course, the savagery of the Muslim fundamentalists transcends all limits of space, time and societal parameters. Is it not a despicable joke that a rapist father-in-law would suddenly become the husband and the raped woman has to accept her own husband as son? What would happen if a grandfather rapes a three-year-old child? Would she become the wife of her grandfather? And her father would be treated as her son? How can her mother be treated as her daughter-in-law? This appears to be their kind of social dispensation.

Our limbs get paralysed when we hear of such incidents. Such mindless games were played with Gudiya as well. 'Can't live with this husband; have to live with the other husband'. Nobody considered Gudiya's wishes or her likes and dislikes. Why should they? Women are nothing but lump of flesh; they are supposed to be devoid of their brains. What is the value of their willingness or unwillingness? Same thing has happened with Imrana. There is no one there to heed to her wishes. She is a victim of the limitless lust of her rapist father-in-law, uncouth decision of the *panchayat* and incredible incivility of the Muslim Law Board. Intoxicated by masochism and religious fundamentalism, men are playing games with her. Probably, it is better to describe it as machismo games rather than a crude game. Acts of naked masochism are more fearsome. Males play such games with a view to assuming power to crush women under their feet. Boys shout when they win games: 'we have won today, hip-hip-hurray!' They do not play such transient games when they grow up. Adult men prefer a permanent settlement, an arrangement to be able to play *ad infinitum*. That is an arrangement for permanent enjoyment and indulgence. Political and economic power, societal and religious sanctions are all centralized in the hands of men. Women have made unlimited sacrifices and undergone unlimited forbearance to help men to monopolize these powers. What are women for if they do not pauperize themselves to make men glorified and powerful? Women have become ideal women by believing in such trash definition created by men. What can be done if men push, stifle, kick, burn, bury, drown and make mincemeat of women? No one has any right to point a finger.

'Imrana is not ours, she is their's.' Therefore, 'they' can do anything with Imrana. Such sentiments are expressed by non-Muslims rather nonchalantly. The moot question is; who are they? It is said, they are Musalmans. It means Imrana is a Muslim property and she has to be a victim of Muslim religious prescriptions. She would have not been martyred like this if she were a Hindu, a Christian, a Buddhist, a Jain or a Jew and not a Muslim. India has, for different religious communities, different set of laws based on religion. These laws have been reformed aeons ago. For example, Hindu males are prohibited from polygamy and their women are not deprived of their property rights. But the laws of the 7th Century still hang on the heads of Muslims. These have not been modified for ages. Whether they like it or not, Indian Muslims are forced to accept these rotten outdated laws obediently. However, in certain Muslim countries in the region, *Shari'ah* laws have been considerably modified. In those countries men cannot divorce by uttering *talaq* thrice, and even if they want they cannot keep four wives at a time. The *Shari'ah* laws are being reformed in Islamic countries. But no one cares for such reforms in India.

Today, Imrana has to take shelter under criminal and civil courts to save her from the tyranny of Islamic laws. A rapist father-in-law cannot be brought to justice under Islamic law. There is no punishment, rather, there are dispensations for rewarding people like him. The raped woman is offered to the penis of the rapist. This endows the rapist with unbridled power to ravish the distressed woman any time he likes. Imranas get justice from the Indian legal system, but religious laws continue to victimize them. While one set of laws saves them, the other maims them. What is the justification of maintaining uncivil laws besides the civilized legal system? What is the purpose of unleashing inequality along with equality? Are we gaining anything by hanging ourselves in uncertain balance just for the sake of peaceful coexistence? Certain ill-purported men might gain by lording over women. But women *per se* are suffering by such actions. Half the humanity is suffering. Innumerable possibilities are dying. It is better to have a uniform law in which the guilty would be punished and the innocents would get justice.

Many are opposed to this. Some jihadi Muslim fundamentalists and populist leaders prefer *status quo*. 'The Muslims want *Shari'ah* laws and they should be provided with that.' There is no one to deeply examine why they want this and whether any one is benefiting from this. Do the educated and conscientious Muslims want this kind of law? Whether the Muslims had opted for these laws if they were educated in scientific stream of learning? Is anyone examining if the Muslim personal, family and succession laws are violating the human rights, or equal rights of women, and whether these laws are satisfying all the conditions offered by democracy? Who cares to note if womenfolk and only womenfolk remain the prime victims of religious acts and laws?

It is a watertight 'they' and 'we' situation. What can we do if the Musalmans dig their own graves? Our survival is the main criterion. Such irresponsible pronouncements are made even by intellectuals. However, they always forget that their own survival would be at stake if Muslims do not survive. If we want to survive it has to be survival in togetherness. The Musalmans are really digging their graves with hardest possible spade and pike axe. Very few of the grave-diggers are conscious of the pit they are digging. The unenlightened believe this is the tunnel to their heaven. The most regrettable fact is that, we, who assume to have survived, do not try to understand that the same tunnel is meant for our journey too, not to heaven but to hell. Those who dig grave today for themselves would not preserve these for their own burial; they would continue to dig grave for others as well. The so-called insulated people are also likely to slip into those graves dug by the fundamentalists. Simply because the soil is one, isn't it?

In fact, different laws for different communities divide a nation permanently. They remain segregated and disjointed. They do not ever get connected. Never can they be enwrapped by the garland of love and care. We would continue to live separately as creatures of different planets till we start living together. It cannot be otherwise. It is well neigh impossible to earn expertise in free evaluation of the people who have been split from the mainstream. They suffer from the schizophrenia of the crisis of identity. This schizophrenic paranoia forces them to project religion as their main totem of identity. Gradually, they get intoxicated by religion and become unconscious intolerant fundamentalists.

The BJP is talking about a uniform civil code. The so-called secularists are opposed to this idea. They are opposed to the BJP, and so they will have to oppose whatever the BJP says—they have decided on this and so they oppose the idea of a uniform civil code. They will not want to accept the idea even if there are thousands of grounds for agreeing to it. Why? Because, the BJP is advocating it. Would the opposing camp assert that the sun rises in the west just to oppose the BJP, because the BJP believes that the sun rises in the east? Many people think that by observing a common civil code, the Muslims have to toe Hindu laws. We are not talking about Hindu laws or any other laws based on religion. By uniform civil code, I mean sets of laws framed on the basis of equal rights, in which religion does not play any role, and which ensure equal rights for men and women. For a civilized democratic country, such sets of codes devoid of any religious tinge or bias are of paramount necessity. The country that guarantees human rights to some and denies the same to some others cannot be flaunted as democratic. All right thinking people should realize that religion-based codes are anathema to democracy, human rights and rights and privileges of women.

The majority community would point finger at the Imranas till such time they are considered as daughters of the others and not daughters of ours, and not daughters of India. They would never treat Imrana's misfortune as theirs. And as they would not identify themselves with Imrana, they would not protest. They would remain aloof out of fear of being branded as anti-Muslim. Well, the stamp of secularism and non-communalism is earned easily by simply accepting such barbarian acts. That is an easy way to earn acclaims. That is pocketing platitudes by shutting down the brains, eyes, ears and other sensory organs. Well! They may be branded as secular but what happens to the country! What happens to the country if 15 crore people languish in darkness and are not left with anything but bad and biased education, bigotry and poverty? This segment will naturally be plagued by the swindlers, rapists, thugs, rouges, terrorists and such other disturbing elements. Is there any one around who has foresight? Any statesman? For the security and unity of the country, it is imperative to introduce secular education by dumping religious edits. It is imperative to replace *Shari'ah* laws by a common civil code. The lurking fear about the future of India would not dissipate till the leaders of the people realize that there is the need to replace darkness with light. A country cannot have a healthy civil society only by implementing economic advancement. Had it been so then Saudi Arabia would have been a paradise for human rights, democracy and women's emancipation.

India does not lag behind in humanitarian activities. Movements are in abundance to save some or to protect someone else. Several laws are there to protect diverse interests. But there are no laws or movements in India to save Muslim women from harassment, indignity, insult and even death. The life of a blackbuck deer is more valuable in India than the lives of eight crore Muslim women. There are laws to save the blackbuck deer, but not for saving any Muslim women.

When a baby is born, it has no religion. The child is forced to conform to the religion of its parents. Even with growth of consciousness, she/he does not accrue the right to choose any other religion or switch over to atheism. Are Shah Banos, Imranas, Latifuneesas and Gudiyas sinners because they were born of Muslim parents? How can the state trample upon their rights as citizens of the country? Why would they be deprived of democratic rights, human rights, freedom of speech, right to equality and security assured under the statutes? What is their fault? Today, these women are shackled, imprisoned behind dark veils and immersed in socio-religious dirt. And these women are not theirs, they are ours; our Swati, Saraswati, Draupadi, Parvati, Sweta and Mahasweta. To me, a single woman imprisoned means imprisonment of womanhood. Women are restrained and constrained in this very country and fie upon those women who consider themselves free while living in this very country! No woman is free when all women are not free. When would this truth dawn in women? What, of course, can they do even if this realization dawns on them? Women are imprisoned in different sizes of cages—small, medium and big. What can they do against heartless and cruel masochistic society? They can shout. Shouting may not achieve anything else, but it gives the satisfaction of shouting. If only all women could jointly chorus a loud bang! I wish they could free themselves of their self-imposed sense of happiness and false freedom from the cardinal mistake that they are safe and secured.

India could have been an example of a true democracy and inspire the neighbours to follow it. Why only the neighbours? Its example could have been followed by the Middle East. India, so big a country, with so much economic strength and unparallel potential, is standing with its head held high. This country could have borne the responsibility of spreading civilization. Who else will do it if the elders do not come forward?

At a convention in Kolkata some years ago, uniform civil code was demanded. All those who belonged to the platform were Muslims. Giasuddin, Sultana Wazeda, Mozaffar Hossein, Sulekha Begum, Zahanara Khatun, Fatema Rehman, Golum Yazdani, Mohabbat Hossein and many others. Can the government not consider these educated, conscious, conscientious, rational people, those who believe in humanity, human rights, democracy and secularism as the representatives of the Muslim society instead of some militants? Then the whole scenario would have changed. Then we could dream of a future free of discrimination. Then the measures to implement other demands of the platform like ensuring human rights, women rights, education free of religion and establishing a society free of religious terror also could have initiated without any disturbance.

This is not a big demand. These demands are meagre. Demands for just a little more civilized society. It is not an irrational demand. A just demand. Do they, who reject it, for a society without discrimination and bigotry? Do they want advancement of the nation?

***

11

Good Wishes to Brothers

I

Recently the ceremony of *Bhai-phonta* for the propitiation of brothers was being performed in many households in Kolkata. Some of my acquaintances insisted me to arrange *Bhai-phonta* for them. I said to those 'brothers': "You first arrange for a *Bon-phonta* for the welfare of the sisters. For ages, there has been enough of *Bhai-phonta* for your welfare. Now do something for the well being of sisters. Change the system." My 'brothers' seemed to have fallen from the sky. They had never heard of such inauspicious thing in their life before.

II

I don't observe Id, Durga Puja, Christmas, etc., since I do not practice any religion. But I receive a lot of mails wishing me

Happy Vijaya, Happy Diwali, etc. These messages were out-numbered by Id Mubarak. Is this because I hail from a Muslim background? It's a fact that I was born of Muslim parents but it doesn't mean that I must be a Musalman. I am out and out an atheist. But there is no practice in our society to appreciate an atheist. Here people are accustomed to classify people by one religion or the other. Those who know well about my atheism do refer to Muslim festivals and rituals before me as 'your Id, your *roza*, your *Shab-e-Barat*' and so on. In fact, man has forgotten to distinguish between the pure and impure. People around me do not believe in my words that I am an atheist and suspect that at the core I am a Muslim. I try to convince them that I practice what I believe in. But I fail to convince them. Perhaps they have not seen a true atheist before. There is no dearth of people who claim to be atheists and still argue that Puja and Id are not religious festivals. They claim those to be social festivals and so they involve themselves in them. That confuses a lot of people. Or, it is so that they are not confused, they fail to realize that it is possible to dissociate oneself from religion and ceremonies linked with religion.

III

The men who have ever dined at my home are in my eyes actu-ally very weak, however robust their appearances may be. I say this because they cannot help themselves with the plates. They keep waiting with empty plates for some woman to arrive and serve them rice and curry. I had announced that at my place it was a self-service lunch. The men then tried to pour rice and curry into their plates, but nobody could manage things properly. They made a mess of the dinner by dropping food on the floor, tumbling the bowls and trays from the table. This happens only with the men, and not with the women. Why? I have cracked the secret. When I had paid visits to my friends' houses, I found that at lunch or dinner, the female members wait at the table to serve their male counterparts. They do not eat until the male members and the guests finish eating. Like slaves they wait behind their males in servitude to see what they need. The males who are antagonist of women's liberty, or the males who are protagonist of women's liberty, both fill their stomach in the same way and belch. The primitive notion 'if women eat before their men, it will bring ill omen to their husbands' still prevails in the 21st Century as well. No pretext to make them eat together works.

IV

Whenever I attend a party in a house in Kolkata, I have noticed to my amazement how all the women gather at one corner and chit-chat while their male counterparts gossip in another corner. One day it slipped out of my tongue: "What's the matter, are you all homosexuals here?" I tried hard to bring the two groups together but the bonhomie did not last long. The subjects the two groups discuss are also different. One group is not much interested in the other group's topic. Women's interests centre round apparel, children, cooking, husbands, household affairs, and at best music. The men talk on politics, economics, sex, money, etc. Even 50 years ago, it was not much different from today. With the passage of time, lots of things have changed for the better, yet the topic of their discussions have not changed. I don't understand why all of them should not talk on the same issues. As a matter of fact, the evolutionary progress has taken place just on the branches and leaves of the tree, but their roots are still far from the taste of a change.

V

Women compulsorily earn some bad reputation in their lifetime. I am not lucky enough to see a woman without a bad name of this or that kind. Men also earn infamy, but it enhances their reputation in the society. I give some examples of men's apparent bad names that actually boost his social prestige: 'He is a great philanderer.' 'He sleeps with many women and cares little for his wife.' 'His maid servant is very sexy and he does it with her everyday.' 'This man has managed pretty well from his in-laws.' 'That man can drink lots of peg in one sitting. He starts early in the morning and continues till late night. Ganja and Heroine are a child's play to him.'

Can you imagine these epithets to be used about women?

VI

I have earned two types of bad reputations. One is that I hate males. I'm a misandrist. The second that I am a misogynist. I hate females. I am now apprehending a third one—that I hate the eunuchs! I have given up minding about these; and now I find that I'm not even worried about my reputation as well. That's better.

VII

In many Indian cities, women are seen riding motorcycles. In Kolkata, however, it's a rare sight. Here only males ride motorcycles. The cyclists wear helmets and the male pillion riders also put on helmets. But if the pillion rider happens to be a woman, she travels without a helmet. A female rides the bike without a helmet, thereby risking her life. Her husband or boyfriend is well protected with a helmet because he is like a god. If there is an accident, the husband will survive, but she will go to heaven with vermilion on her forehead. There is no parallel to a woman in her preparedness to sacrifice her own life to save the life of her husband or boyfriend.

***

12

Civilized Laws at Last

Torturing women was like waking up in the morning, like urinating after waking up, like brushing one's teeth, like enjoying a cup of tea. It was like buying a pack of cigarettes, like boarding a bus, like going to the office, like taking a nap after lunch. Like gossiping, like consuming *khoini*, like having two pegs in the evening, like watching cricket on TV. Like going to bed scratching one's thigh after having dinner and belching. Atrocities on women were such innocent, insignificant thing. So mundane, so normal.

Suddenly something has happened.

Suddenly the law-babu has come down to the villages, threatening everyone that dire consequences would have to be faced if anyone turned wicked. In this country of wicked without a warning law-babu has come down with his red eyes wielding stick. Seeing him, the male crowd has come out witl tridents in their hands. They are on sexual strike with red flags tied with their penises. They will not eat a grain before driving the law-babu out. All about one hears hissing of envy. Those who look like gentlemen are saying, "Nothing can be achieved by making laws. The law that cannot be enforced is just a mockery of law." Some others are grimacing and saying, "This is not a law, this is a fatwa." Someone claims that in a modern society it is better to regulate the least. Society will change by its internal needs. Not by diktats from outside.

There is no dearth of people who call this rotten old society filled with superstition a modern society. It is amazing that a fanatic patriarchal society is considered a modern society. Here, men still come to 'choose the would-be bride'. After marriage the women are sent to the in-law's house. They have to wear *sankha* and use *sindur* and change their title to denote that they are someone's property. Men are, however, not supposed to carry any symbol marking them as married.

In this 'modern' society, wives are victims of all sorts of torture, physical and mental. Female foeticide continues; one faces abuses if one cannot give birth to a son; a widow has to spend a very bitter life. But a man whose wife has died does not undergo any hardship. In this modern society both the husband and the wife go out to work, but after returning home the wife has to serve like a slave, while the man becomes a husband, a master. The more society is modernized, the more women turn into commodity. They have to be in perfect size and clothes to satisfy man's physical and mental needs. Here rape, killing of wives and torturing them continues with impunity. In this modern society, girls humiliated and ignored for their dark skin commit suicide.

If this is definition of modernity, then even if doomsday appear it would still remain almost impossible to reform this society.

Society does not turn modern if women get some degrees from colleges and universities, wear skimpy clothes and dance at discotheques, or drink and smoke.

This society is not modern. It reeks of inequality. Compromises mark family life. Compromises do not make modernity. It is peaceful cohabitation of masters and slaves.

The husbands are raping their wives days after days. Now if that rape is considered rape, who objects to that? The rapists. Those innumerable people are seething in anger. 'Can't we have sex with our wives? Done it by force? Yes, but with my wife. Not with the boys and girls walking on the street. My wife is my property. I can do whatever I like with her. Why should anyone interfere in it? This law is aimed at destroying family peace."

As those men believe that women are their property, so also the women who are treated as so. That is how without any reason or rationale marriages are continuing. Now the law-babu has come with objections on acting freely with my property. But what does the legal system in India say? Does not it say I have right to my property?

How many people know that women are not property of men? Some know, but do they follow it? Society is patriarchal. We should not forget that society is patriarchal. Men control it. If some women show 'manliness' and try to curb the powers of men that does not mean men are women's property.

'Laws will not be implemented'—one should not banter the laws like this. In a dark society, time may be required for full implementation of laws. Initially, women may be shy about taking recourse to it. They will be scared of rogues and people's hatred. They will be threatened. But someday it will be implemented. Someday some will come forward to demand justice under the law. When pushed to the corner, they will ignore the threats of men to come forward. Watching them, some more women will become bold and join them. It cannot be so that wicked men will go scot free for ever. They will have to be trapped and the law is the means to do that. Otherwise, they will slip away. So long laws protected the wicked and allowed them to slip away.

'Laws will remain in the statute book, and there will be no implementation of them'—those who claimed so were proved wrong the day after the encoding of the law when in Tamil Nadu one Joseph was arrested for beating his wife. He had to get himself released after paying 20,000 rupees as fine. What the Joseph could do so long would not be tolerated any more. If love could create a situation of peaceful coexistence, that could have been ideal. If that does not happen, one has to depend on fear. Peace is to be ensured by the terror factor. This is a pious race, and the fear of religion keeps it somewhat soft.

There is no reason why the two-legged animal called human beings would not become violent if it hungry, or envious, or angry. But people learn to suppress many such desires through moral education imparted to them from after their birth. If the males have grown up with the education that committing atrocities against women is not wrong, then they will have to be educated in this way. By law.

Don't hurt the others, don't harm the others, don't beat the others—many such laws are there. But there is no practise of including women among 'the others'. Why should not there be laws for protecting, for giving security to women? Particularly those women who are compelled to live with males as their wives, fiancées, mothers, daughters and so on.

When there are same laws for a married couple and a couple living together, it denotes that society is making short steps towards modernity. But this law is for people of all religions. It is not written in the law that it is only for the Hindus, the Christians and the Santhals. So this is for all. But what will happen when it will clash with the Muslim personal laws at each step? Which side the people will take—the side of justice or injustice?

The males have turned crazy; but for them it will not be so easy to get rid of this law as the men thought of. The urgency of this law is being felt in all the nooks and corners of cities and ports and villages. Some say taking recourse to this law against the head of the family will increase quarrels, violence, misunderstanding and jealousy. As though now there is no such thing, as though now it is only love that dominates.

But the law on atrocities have not solved all the problems of women. After divorce, women come out without anything. They may get back only what was paid as dowry. But things are not divided in halves. When will the law-babu come forward for that? He has many more things to do, many more things. When he has come once, he should not harm humanity by fleeing from the scene facing abuses and tridents of men.

***

13

Mahashweta, Medha, Mamata
Great Women of Great Universe

Women know nothing about politics, do not understand economics, do not understand cricket and cannot perform difficult tasks. Women cannot do, women do not know, women do not understand. I keep hearing this all the time. But women have proved time and again that they know, they can do, they understand. Not just that, they know a lot more than men, understand more and perform better. Nonetheless, women fall victim to the conspiracy of a misogynistic society. Men are ensconced comfortably in their seats, having denied all of women's knowledge and ability by sheer brute force. Women have been dumped with the task of making all arrangements for the ease and comfort of men. Women will remain backstage, behind the scenes. Behind everybody, beneath everybody, amidst the proletariat. Some women, however, break the rules prescribed by men and come forward. They prove in times of crisis that they are the ones to turn to. Mamata, Mahashweta and Medha, these three women whatever be their political ideology, whatever the mistakes they may have made in life, have stood by the people during hard times, have risked major mishaps, but never compromised with forces of ruthlessness. There is no truth greater than this. There is no humanity greater than this.

A woman removes boulders strewn on the road. A man comes and walks along that very road like a king. Man sits on the throne and rules over the state. When men create anarchy, when they create disorder, when they fight wars, when they kill, it is women who come forward holding high the banner of peace. In every home, women are confronting men who are thieves, robbers, drunkards, lumpens and murderers; women are restraining them, transforming them, making them human. Women are suffering in order to give warmth to others. It may appear from this aspect of women that they are born only to serve and give. But it is not so; women can also fight wars, and indeed do so. Women too can become nasty and hideous. They can become despotic rulers. History stands testimony to it. It is not as if woman is synonymous with the emblem of peace. Women are no less capable of destruction, brutality and murder.

It is women who uphold peace within the house and outside it. All religions, nevertheless, declare that women are the gateway to hell. Men and the patriarchal system have only irreverence, neglect, disease and suffering to offer to women. Politics keeps women at arm's length. How many women today are ministers? How many women are members of Parliament? How many women are in the Politburo? How many women are there in administration? How many women hold top posts in academics? But of course, it is not long since women's education have begun! The entire society was against education of women till the other day. Aren't there people who are against women's education even today? Certainly yes! Isn't it still believed that boys should be sent to school, not girls? That it is better to teach girls to cook and keep in house and then marry them off? When girls are indeed sent to school, is it really for the sake of getting them educated? It is only to enhance their prospects in the marriage mart! Urban people think that girls in cities are highly educated. Alas! Even after passing out of schools, colleges and universities, do many people know that man and woman are both human beings and that they have equal rights? Educated, urban girls take their children to school and stand in front of the school gate all day. What does the child learn at the end of the day?

Over the years, apart from mathematics-science-history-geography, do they ever learn that the rights and liberties of both men and women are equal? And what about those girls who hold ten-to-five jobs? Do they know? They humbly obey all orders and instructions of their male masters. Sitting down when asked to, on the bed when asked to. Their merit has no value, their skill is worth nothing. Women are not even allowed to work night and day and earn a living. It is not just at the workplace, things are the same at home too. They must not just work hard, but sacrifice a lot too. They must sacrifice their self-respect, dignity, personality—everything that teaches one to hold one's head high. In this society, no one is wiling to recognize a woman as 'good' unless she is willing to make sacrifices. So a

woman must sacrifice her all if she is to be enlisted as 'good'. I
believe there is no difference between being enlisted as 'good'
and enlisted as a prostitute.

There is nothing that women cannot do. They can stir up
trouble if they wish to, they can bring in peace if they wish to.
Just as they can love, so can they hate. Whenever men have let
the world decay, women have come forward to stem the rot.
They have raised crops. Everything has been sprinkled with amity
and affection. Keeping women behind the screen, men have
grabbed the credits time and again. It is women who create, who
construct, and it is men who enrich themselves with the bond of
brotherhood. Is there any such word for women? Sisterhood? No,
there isn't. There is neither the custom, nor the practice. Women
are wrenched apart from each other. From mothers, from sisters,
from friends. Women's link with the other women is destroyed
time and again. From the beginning of history, female bonding
has been destroyed by religions, by systems, by incantations.
Women are bound by men, but there is no way women can
create bond with women. If a woman shouts out loud when
denied her rightful due, there is no way for a hundred women
to join in chorus, no way a thousand women will shout out with
her. Women have no strong organization. Whatever exists is for
groups of middle-aged housewives or almost-housewives who
meet once a month or once a year, hum among themselves and
are either struck spellbound by the extent of their freedom, or
simply faint in wonder.

Men have created the definition of a beautiful woman. Going
by that definition, women dress up like lunatics—they have

to exhibit themselves as beautiful, or else they will be left with no prestige, they will have no worth in society. A major part of the little money that a self-reliant woman earns is spent on stuff needed for dressing up. Much of the little time she has to herself is spent on investigation—what should she wear or not wear in order to appear attractive to people. Men have indeed given women a good job with which to remain busy—a huge task apart from cooking, raising kids and keeping house. Woman should be so busy that she does not have the time to understand politics or economics. She should not have even the little time required to understand cricket.

There is simply no question of her beginning to understand the ABC of her rights. So many handicaps, so many obstacles! A hundred snares of conspiracy. All arrangements are in place to crush women till they are annihilated. Even after all this, it is women who are seen standing with their spine erect. It is in this misogynistic society that fearless women like Mahashweta, Medha and Mamata are born.

We can surely hope for more Mahashwetas, more Medhas! Woman does have the talent (*medha*) to be a Medha. Woman does have the compassion (*mamata*) to be a Mamata. She has the power to be a Mahashweta. Then why woman should lag behind, why should she remain a housewife? Why she sits content as a mere mother! Why does she remain lifeless, dumb, listless, lusterless, dull, insensate, weak, indifferent, silent and banned! Woman does know how to be a raging fire. Then why does she not start a fire! A fire in which every single discrimination in society may burn to ashes!

It is women who have stretched out their hands to turn hard times into good times. Let those hands be joined with hundred thousand hands that had grinded spice, cleaned rice, used the needle-and-thread, the hands that had raised children, had wielded the pen, used the hammer and the chisel, the sickle and the spade. Let all the hands of all women come together.

***

14
Women: Dauntless Courage and Determination

The girls who used to pass their lives in taciturnity are today boldly facing police atrocities at Singur. The women who never came out of their homes, who never saw the dazzling street lights of Kolkata, are observing fasts for a mission. Men are also fasting. But, after coming back from Singur, a friend said: "The men are apprehensive of retribution for anti-government stance; but fasting women are displaying terrific courage and determination. They are saying, do or die. So much determination and courage!" Where did they get it from? Twenty-year-old to 75 years of age—they are all alike. No one will compromise, or make a retreat. It's a pleasant surprise for me. It reminds me of women of the western countries, who came out on the streets to acquire their right to vote. They had to withstand police atrocities, but they never gave in. It is reminiscent of the role of women in freedom struggles in different countries. Men made compromises, but women did not. This determination, courage and resolution that we are now hearing of—where do these characters go afterwards? When they slip into the confines of four walls, they are throttled, shackled. In spite of their determination and dauntless courage, they rot in homes. Only in time of anarchy in the country, they become visible. They are at the front of a procession. They are those who have discarded their veils and *burqas*. Then who is imprisoning them in homes? Why are they not able to break free from the strong walls of the prison facing themselves? If someone had snatched away the hammer from their hands, can't they snatch it again? Can't they collect another hammer for breaking the prison walls? Where do they lose such honesty, truthfulness and will power? Who kills these qualities? We know the answer. Still most of us keep mum and pretend ignorance.

The question that haunts me now is whether the land acquired by the government at Singur ever belonged to these women? Or did it belong to their fathers, husbands, brothers? Nothing belongs to women, nothing is for their welfare; yet the land or wealth is protected by their assistance. Women safeguard everything. But hardly do they care for any hard times that they may find themselves in. Their capacity to take risks is greater than anybody else on this earth. This has been proved by them time and again. Taking great risks, they have achieved the unachievable. Nevertheless their firmness and straightforwardness have been belittled by vile patriarchs in homes and outside.

Men fight battles. When they win battles, they maraud the wealth of the defeated soldiers. They capture enemy's home and hearth, property and women. Since ancient times, this has been the way of the world for men. Men have never acknowledged independent identity of women. Women have always been men's property. Men believe they have the right to do whatever they like to do with their property. Women are the worst victims of wars. Though they do not take part in wars, they are killed, raped, made refugees, orphans, lonely, and totally ruined. Men are not as much affected by war as women are. Men are killed in wars and the wives and children of the belligerent men have to lead miserable lives. Nobody can share their misery.

I am against wars. The world is being flooded with inhuman objects like atomic bombs. If the expenditure on the production of deadly weapons is slightly curtailed, we can use the money saved from it for food, education and health of all the poor people living on this earth. But why will the warmonger men do that? There is no dearth of clamour for peace. Interestingly, the more men fight wars, the more peace prizes are bagged by them! But they do nothing for peace. These days again, peace prizes have become the pets of the capitalists. One can win peace prizes even after cheating and oppressing the poor and accumulating wealth without hindrance. Men are fond of weapons, arsenal, wars, violence and bloodshed.

Though I do not personally admire David Eisenhower, the former US President, yet I agree fully with what he said, that the money required for each gun, rocket and war, is the money stolen from those who are starving, who are suffering from cold and without clothes.

That day I was walking around Rabindra Sadan and Nandan. A programme of dance was going on in Rabindra

Sadan. A couple of thousand were present to watch it. A little distance away from there, five to six people were squatting on the ground at a meeting organized by a human rights group to protest the police atrocities at Singur. I felt depressed at the sight. So many people in music and dance, but so few in a protest meeting, so few for human rights! Do men no more cry for men? Nevertheless, I should say, the people of West Bengal have assembled and registered their points of view on the issue of Singur. Everybody wants peace. At least most of the people, if not all. Barring the most ruthless, nobody wants oppression to be unleashed on the poor. I am happy to think the people of West Bengal are large-hearted.

There are two kinds of wars in this world. One is by the oppressor against the oppressed. The other one is by the oppressed against the oppressor. I have always been a supporter of the second one. So amidst hundreds of perils, I take side with the oppressed. I do not want oppression to continue on earth. I do not want discrimination and injustice to prevail. I want rights and freedom. I want peace. It is far easier to establish peace than to wage wars. But this easy thing is not being done. Complex crooked men, the weapon-mongers object to this simple task. They who wield power have their human compassionate eyes eaten by vultures.

Voltaire once said, "It would be easier to subjugate the entire universe through force than the minds of a single village." These words of Voltaire remind me of the people of Singur. Perhaps the Tatas will set up their motor factory at Singur. People will gradually forget about the hunger strike of those women, about the police atrocities on them. But the mind of the tiny village will remember for ever the gloomy days it has passed through. The sad tales of the women of Singur will perhaps not impress the historians. They will exclude from their books the display of courage and determination of women, their participation in hunger-strike, loud protestations and courting risks. History is written by men. Will they, the men of this anti-woman society that has not learnt to show respect to women, remember women, or their acts of bravery? The women will pass into oblivion finding no place in the pages of history.

Political leaders boast of patriotism. Intellectuals enjoy sporting their love for the country. But no one is perhaps more efficient than these people in compromising with what is false and untrue. Even President Roosevelt once commented: "It's unpatriotic not to tell the truth, whether about the president or anyone else." Musical soirees, state-sponsored poetry festivals are attended by countless number of poets reading gleefully their poems of love and languishment. The noted poets have locked their mouths while the procession in protest against the acquisition of land for motor factory at Singur is passing by them. They are silent because they fear retributive action. But will their loss be greater than that of the girls on hunger strike in Singur? Will there ever be more harm to those famous urban poets than that of the women of Singur?

Long, long ago Voltaire had said: "It is dangerous to be right when the government is wrong." Even today, in every step of our life, this saying is as much relevant as it was in the past. It is women who are taking the risk of life at every stage. Only women will die in the hunger strike. Perhaps men will withdraw their hunger strike but not women. If these perfect, bold, honest and courageous women had ruled the state, nation or even the world, the earth would have been a lovelier place to live in.

***

15

Let Girls Seethe in Rage and Anger

Has a day passed without any incident of rape? No. No such day. A survey conducted in 2000 revealed that in India at least one woman is raped every hour. Actually, this figure would have been much more dismal if all rape survivors had come forward to report. Most people do not know that rape is a crime. The rapist is not recognized as a criminal, the rape victim is. For a society nothing can be more shameful. Rape is the only crime in the world where the victim is regarded as the offender.

American feminist writer Marilyn French wrote: "All men are rapists and that's all they are. They rape us with their eyes, their laws and their codes."

And my favourite Andrea Dawkins said: "As long as there is something called rape in this world, there will be no peace or justice or equality or liberty. You can never become what you want to become, you can never live in the world you want to live in." He further said: "Rape is no accident, no mistake. In a patriarchal culture rape is the definition of sexuality. As long as this definition exists, men will be recognized as sexual aggressors and women as their victims. Those who think this culture to be natural, carry out rapes every day in cold blood."

There are some who say that rapists ought to be castrated. That will soon put an end to rape. But will it really stop rape? Wasn't there any rape in this state on the very next day after Dhananjoy was hanged? There was. Why? There are stringent laws against rape. But has that restricted the number of rapes? Those fools who say that girls in skimpy dresses themselves are provocation for men to rape them, know fully well that girls draped from head to toe, even girls in *burqa* are raped ever so often. Clothes are not the issue here: the issue is the male organ. Right from birth, men have learnt that they can win the world with that 2 or 3-inch long, functional or dysfunctional bit of thing hanging between their thighs. Men get this lesson everywhere: in schools, in colleges, streets, workplaces, business establishments, through laws, in cities and ports, in the functioning of the state, the province, their homes and society. How many men dare to cast aside this teaching which they get at home and outside and which men have practised for a thousand years?

Some years ago, an incident took place in Bangladesh. A 15-year-old girl called Yasmin worked as a domestic help in the house of a middle class family living in Dhaka. The head of the house raped her every night. One night, Yasmin escaped from the house. She made straight for parents' place. On the way, she was accosted by the police. 'Where are you going?' they asked. 'To my father's house,' she replied. 'Your house is a long way off. Get into the car, we will drop you off.' Then the police car stopped in the desolate darkness. Seven policemen raped Yasmin to their heart's content. Then they strangled her to death and dumped the body in a garbage heap. The next day local people took out a procession against the police. The police fired on the procession. Seven villagers died. The following day, an official press release declared that Yasmin was a depraved woman, the police were right in doing whatever they did. Do such incidents happen only in Bangladesh? Don't they happen anywhere else? We all know they do. All the time the protector turns out to be the devourer. And why not? Devouring a woman is not an offence! Woman is meant to be enjoyed, consumed and devoured. Everybody knows this and accepts it as such. Everybody from a priest to a five-year-old boy knows that man is omnipotent. And it is their supreme right to trample on women, to subjugate them; it is their supreme right to rape women when they please, to persecute them beyond endurance, to burn them to death.

When this will stop, evil times will be dispelled for ever. In this society, there is no tradition of respecting women. The definition of 'respect' made by men is tantamount to disrespect of women.

Robin Morgan, editor of the famous feminist magazine *Ms.*, said a lot of important things on rape. He said: "Performance of the sexual relation that is not initiated by a woman, that which does not take place out of the true sexual desire of a woman, is tantamount to the performance of rape."

In a sexual relationship existing in a patriarchal atmosphere, and within the control of the male, there is no reason why there should not be, not just discrimination, but untold oppression as well. It is but inevitable when there is discrimination and male domination all around. Even the most abominable monstrosity is condoned if it is performed behind closed doors and given the name of 'love making'.

Robin Morgan further said, "Rape is the perfected act of male sexuality in a patriarchal culture. It is the ultimate metaphor for domination, violence, subjugation and possession."

No, our feminists do not put it like this. Never. Very few rapists have escaped from the clutches of the Western feminists. They in the West have fought this abominable, hateful form of oppression of women for a long, long time. They never let off anyone.

Today, in Western countries, where women can live in almost complete freedom, it is very natural for women to take the initiative in love and sexuality. The woman chooses the man, it is she who physically desires the man, expresses her desire and is the more active partner in the sexual act.

In our country, the more passive the woman partner is, the more the man is aroused. Men desire passive women in sexual relationships. Feminists say there is no need for women to achieve sexual rights. Women need education and self-reliance. Indigenous brand of feminism! Well. Do not these feminists know that even after achieving educational and economic self-reliance women remain sexual slaves of men? Or is it so that they refuse to accept this as a fact? Or is it that they surreptitiously nourish patriarchy with water and manure to keep the system alive and fresh!

In this country, women cannot live with their head held high. Women are not supposed to be proud. It was ages back that Elizabeth Cady Stanton, leader of the suffragist movement, had declared, 'We are as a sex infinitely superior to man.' How many girls in the Indian subcontinent believe in and repeat these words?

We women are greater than men in every way: if this is stated, not only men laugh in jest, women too start laughing. Women had always been above men not only as a gender, but also in conscience, intelligence, sagacity, observation, rebellion, or explosion. But this power has been kept in chains for a thousand years now. Is it that simple to break the age-old fetters?

I think abhorrence for men is a respectable political ideology, an ideology that entitles the oppressed to shower hatred on the class of oppressors: But, how many people in this country utter such a thing? This is the age of liberalism. The more you compromise, the better. The more you concede the more tolerant and peace-loving you are. But those who have created unrest over the ages, those who have unrest and disorder seething in every cell of the brain, in every drop of blood, is it possible to have any meaningful peace treaty with them?

Ages back, Marilyn French wrote this in the book, *Women's Room*: "My feelings for men are related to my experiences with them. Truth to tell, I have no sympathy for men. Just as the Jew who has just come out from the Dachau concentration camp, walks away in supreme indifference on seeing a young Nazi soldier writhing in agony after being hit by a bullet in the stomach, so do I feel on seeing a man. I don't even feel it necessary to shrug. I don't care. It does not matter to me what he was like as a human being, what he wished for or what he did not."

How many in this society have the strength or the courage to treat men with contempt? Women will never be liberated from the yoke of patriarchy unless they can treat men with contempt. Our rebellious predecessor women renounced marriage. Does anyone dare to say this: As marriage is to fasten women to shackles of slavery, the aim of feminism should be to give the institution of marriage a hard kick. Unless the institution of marriage is abolished, women's emancipation will never be attained.

'No, no, no. We are marching forward arm in arm with men. We have come a long way. We have long achieved the rights that are our due. For the little that is left, we have to strive with men by our side.' Such an opinion is shared by almost everybody, irrespective of whether they are women or men. But can we fight with rapists by our side? Is there any man who does not boast of that 2 or 3-inch long thing of his? Even those men who call themselves feminists, at times check to confirm the presence of that thing between the thighs. If you put your trust in the race of rapists, you are done for.

Yes, we will talk race. Men belong to a different race. They are different from the human race. No one in our society says such a thing even in anger. Has the rage of girls been extinguished all together? Girls do a lot of things in a moment of intense anger. Why doesn't anybody castrate a rapist and feed the organ to the dogs? Why doesn't white hot anger make girls pronounce the truth—that truth which they are forced to swallow even when it is at the tip of the tongue? That truth which they have had to swallow for a thousand of years? Why can't they say it aloud, even now?

***

16

From One Man to Another

The decision of the Rajasthan High Court astounded me. Rajasthan is known for its bias against women and for its adherence to ancient traditions. It is known as a state where women have enjoyed far less freedom than the women in other states. How could a court in such a state declare that an adult woman has the right to live with her lover, even if her husband was opposed to it!

Incredible! And yet, this has happened. Manju now lives with her lover and not with her husband. Justice GC Mishra and Justice KC Sharma of Rajasthan High Court had ruled that no one should have the right to use a woman as a commodity.

This is a big blow to the institution called marriage. No other institution has witnessed so much conflict as marriage. Other institutions have dented, waned, survived for some time and then burnt out. But not marriage. In the 60s, during the days of the Hippies, it was almost on the dock. But that was in the West, not in the East. Western youths did spurn marriage then. But all that began to change in the 80s. The ogre of conservatism invaded Europe. It always had the East in its clutches.

And now, while in India, I hear that a court here has said no one should force a girl to live with someone against her will! It is as though the time has suddenly leaped a hundred years. And yet, we know nothing much has changed. Rather, that verdict is at odds with this society. It is just a verdict from a good judge. There is no reason to be overenthusiastic about it? I wonder if Manju, who is now living with her lover, is happy? Aren't people yelling curses and invectives at her? Aren't they threatening to lynch her? Aren't they calling her a fallen woman, a slut, a prostitute? We may assume, surely, Manju now shudders in insecurity. She can hardly enjoy her new life of love. And how long will Suresh's love for her last? Isn't he being jeered each day for having usurped 'someone else's wife'? His relatives and neighbours must be sneering at him. How long can one put up with all that? Women perhaps can; they are used to it. All through their lives, they are taught to put up with all these. But a man has got to do what he has got to do to keep his head held high. Suresh being a man will come out of his shell the moment he will face difficulties. What happens if Suresh dumps Manju? Where will she go then? Either she will go back to her husband, or will find a shelter in the house of a new lover. What else?

What is the worth of such solution if a woman must shuttle from one man to another? Is it not far better that she should not need any one's protection, that she alone will be enough for herself, that she could live with honour and confidence, daring and arrogant, without a care for anyone's kindness or pity?

What change a verdict of one court in one state can usher in a society that has never accorded importance to a woman's wishes, where education, health, or self-respect of a girl is not important, where a woman must depend from birth till death on the will of men around her? Society remains what it has been —anti-woman.

And if we probe deeper, it is all the same whether Manju lives with her husband or her lover. At either place, she at best gets a shelter. At either place, she must unconditionally surrender everything she has. Depending on men's whims, she will be kicked or kissed. Her present and her future will depend entirely on the nature and whim of a man. What more insecurity should a woman suffer from? Men bring in maximum insecurity in the lives of women. No one can harm a woman more than men.

No woman is secure till she herself can arrange for her shelter. I know many will angrily retort that all men are not evil, that there are many who are good. I know there are. But such dependence on the goodness of men only adds to the helplessness of a woman. A woman is safe till that goodness lasts. Must a woman keep doing the rounds from a bad man to a better one, and from such a one to a still better one? A woman not only needs to protect herself from man's cruelty and injustice, but also from man's alms—goodness, pity, mercy, and a little kindnesses. Man's pity and mercy are no less cruel than man's torture and injustice. Those small mercies only keep a woman mesmerized. She loses her ability to protest. She turns foolish, and deaf, and dumb, and offers flowers at the feet of men. And that turns men into megalomaniac monsters.

When will women be their own strength? I dream of the day when women will no longer need men's pity and kindness.

I dream of a man-woman relationship to be one like between the prudent intelligent men of mutual respect.

All ugly things of the world like class, sex discrimination, caste and communalism thrive because human beings have no respect for their fellow human beings. One would expect such discrimination to disappear with time and spread of education, and the progress of science. But, the opposite is happening. Human beings are turning more superstitious, more narrow-sighted, and more fanatical.

Among all animals, it is only women who live intimately with her very tormentors. No other creature gives love and service to its tormentor. Women's greatest problem is that they cannot understand and are not allowed to understand that man's shelter is no solution to their problems. A man might shelter her today and abandon her tomorrow, love her today and spurn her tomorrow, see her as beautiful today, only to dub her ugly tomorrow. Women can never trust Men.

And if, by chance, a woman finds a faithful man, she has to give up all to keep him faithful. Most of the time, a woman gains nothing even after sacrificing everything. Many don't even gain an iota of compassion. And no one views that as unjust.

Just men are rare. There are so many luminaries—in politics, economics, trade, science, arts, literature—who ill-treat their wives at home, or go with other women and cheat their wives, or use their wives merely as slaves. Who then can be trusted if such great men cannot be trusted?

Truth is, somewhat like a lottery—you never know who you can trust, and who you cannot; who will cheat you, and who will not. As men never respect women as fellow human beings, women must lose out in the end. Everyone has accepted it as only natural. Beaten and cheated, women still repose their trust in men, and seek their shelter.

If women cannot trust themselves, then against all reason and logic, they will have to place their trust in men. Women suffer a lot for their stupidity, but the worst thing is suffering due to reposing trust in men.

***

17
Feminism, Liberation and Independence!

I

Seventeen years from today, I had written about the Samsad Bengali dictionary. In it the meaning of 'male' was given as 'human being', but in case of 'female', there were other things except 'human beings'. Many people were amazed. They opened the dictionary, and could not believe their eyes. Shockingly, to date, the meaning of the word remains the same.

II

I consider the term male as a negative one. If patriarchy is negative, then why not male? Men have never tried to obliterate the patriarchal system that is surviving for many thousand years. Had they really wanted to do so, they could have done away with this system. For equality and egalitarianism they could have finished off patriarchy. But they did not do so. I want to use the word 'male' as synonym of the words like inconsiderate, narrow-minded, ungrateful, selfish, greedy, avaricious, inferior and envious. I want to abuse them by the term male. I want to abuse those boys and girls who have those traits. I want to say: "Fie!! You're so ugly, so miserly, so dirty, so male!"

III

Males are still the masters of educated, self-dependent ladies of Kolkata. Women are coming to parties, drinking, dancing and saying. "My husband has given me lots of freedom. Very few women enjoy so much freedom!"

Their faces glitter in gratitude. I say to myself: "Freedom is your birthright. It is there with you. Who is he to give it to you?"

Men are sitting on the heads of women. Women also give them the indulgence to sit on their heads. Sitting on their heads, the males eat their brains. They eat it, eat like the insects, and enter into it as insects. They then damage the brain cells. Why don't women firmly shake their heads to throw the men off from their heads? They should say: "Stand beside us, or behind us, but never try to climb on our heads."

IV

Many, even women, ask me, "They call you feminist; why don't you protest?"

Amazed, I reply, "Why should I? I believe in feminism." At this, many look upset. I explain to them, "As I believe in humanism, so I believe in feminism. You cannot be a humanist without being a feminist. How can I? One cannot be a humanist if one keeps mum when one witnesses torture of human beings."

"Women are either feminists, or masochists, who derive pleasure from being hurt," once commented a feminist. I also subscribe to this view. If you don't want to be a masochist, you must be a feminist. I don't want to be tortured, repressed, crushed, or burnt by men and patriarchal society. That's why I am a feminist.

A feminist is one who considers both man and woman as complete human beings and believes in the equal rights and privileges of both.

Most of the people have no clear conception of such a simple ideology like feminism. The faith in equal political, social, economic rights of men and women is feminism—is it something very hard to understand?

Many look upon the term feminism with anger not only in the countries of the southern hemisphere, but in north as well. Some had proposed using a different term in place of feminism, a term that is not controversial. Will a new term solve all the problems? No. Not so. People are not worried about 'feminism'. They worry about the action of the feminists. It matters little whether a woman considers herself a feminist or not. But the determination of a woman to get her rights is a dangerous thing.

Rebecca West, a British writer, had once said that she did not know exactly what was feminism. What she knew was that whenever she expressed her inner self, thereby distinguishing herself from the doormat or the prostitute, people called her feminist.

Author Delve Spender had once written: Feminism does not wage any war, does not kill the opponent, does not build any concentration camp, does not starve the enemy to death, does not indulge in any ruthlessness. It demands education, right to vote, better environment at workplaces, security on the streets, social welfare, welfare of women refugees, reformation of anti-women laws.... If somebody says, 'I'm not a feminist', I ask, 'what is your problem?' So the moot point is: If a woman has no problem with her brain, she must be a feminist.

There are innumerable definitions of feminism. Feminism is a political theory and practice that aims at emancipating all women. All women? Yes, all women—women of black brown yellow skins, the working women, the poor women, the disabled women, the homosexual women, the aged women; not only that, the white, rich, heterosexual women.

Another simple definition of feminism is emphatic statement that women are human beings. 'Feminism is a radical notion that women are human beings.'

This simple definition appears complex to them who are reluctant to honour women as human beings.

V

Women are the only group among the oppressed, who live very closely with their oppressors. Feminists have said lots of things from time to time, but there is very little mention of those in history. All men—of the east, west, north or south—are characteristically same and undistinguishable. Whatever the feminists say from any part of the globe, matches with the experiences of women of the rest of the world.

Men ask for forgiveness because of their weakness, whereas women beg pardon for their strengths. Women of the west have said this. Do the women of the east not know this?

For men, it is normal to be strong and sturdy. For women, it is just the opposite. To be weak and frail is supposed to be a feminine virtue. If she is strong, it is considered a flaw in her character. This is the attitude of the society where we live in. Women are called peaceful and passive. They say it is her innate virtue. No, not so. A woman is a complete human being, and only that is her inborn quality, nothing else.

I am mentally very strong, economically self-reliant and morally an independent person. This is not at all liked by men. They want to see a woman in frailty. Men derive a terrific pleasure from gripping and trampling women under their feet. Nothing gives them greater pleasure than this.

Personally, as I am unwilling to accept the male dominance, I live alone. If a woman is not willing to hurt herself, she is a feminist. If she is a feminist, she will obviously need a home of her own. So many years back in 1928, Virginia Woolf, had written an important book entitled, *A Room of One's Own*. All women require a home of their own. The western women have managed their own homes. Society can no longer scare them. But Indian women still go pale as they face the blood-shot eyes of the society. They are so much frightened that they cannot speak against the oppressive, tyrannical, uncivilized, shameless, ruthless men. Forget about pushing them off from this vicinity, the women treat these men like their loved ones, give them indulgence throughout their lives.

Since the day I am living alone, I have realized the value of my life. Had I lived with a man, it would not have been possible. His life would have become more important. In comparison to a man's life, a woman's life is meaningless, insignificant in this society. If she lives together with the oppressor, she will not get time or opportunity to realize the value of her life. She will have to remain ever busy in providing her male partner service, sexual pleasure and entertainment.

Why do I live alone? Because, I am not a masochist. I do not want to suffer. I do not want a man to trample me under his feet at the slightest opportunity. Outside, they are doing it, but I shall not let them in. I will not allow it under the pretext of any relationship, never in the pretext of a romantic relation like 'living together'.

Liz Winsted, a girl from North America, had once said, "I think, therefore I'm single." Is there any need to add anything to bring home the point why women should live single? If women have grey matter, they should never live with men.

***

18

Whose Defeat is This Really?

A fundamentalist group issued a fatwa against Pakistan tourism minister Nilofar Bakhtiar for hugging her French paratrooper instructor. Nilofar had hoped that the ruling party, PML-Q, would stand by her. But nobody came forward. Nilofar did not receive the support she had expected either from her party or the government.

An Indian television channel had organized a talk show a day after the *fatwa* was issued against Nilofar. The participants of the show were in different countries and in different regions. But technology brought them all together. There was Asma Jahangir, human rights activist from Pakistan, *fatwa* victim Nilofar Bakhtiar, and myself from India. Asma Jahangir said that in Pakistan, fatwas against women were issued everyday, but the media was now highlighting the issue because the victim was a minister, and that was why there was such hue and cry all around. Nilofar rejected it as anything significant. She said that a tiny group had issued the fatwa, no one knew them and neither their words nor the fatwa was worth anything. People would just ignore them. Her party was supporting her, so were the government and the people. She was ready to do what she did all over again.

However, I said that the group in question should not be ignored merely because it was a small group. Since the terrible power that worked behind every fatwa was religion, it did not matter if the person issuing the fatwa was an insignificant wretch. As it had the consent of religion, all buggers would support the fatwa, and the giants of patriarchy will nod their heads in unbounded joy. If measures are not taken to separate religion from the state, if laws are not enacted on the basis of equal rights, if madrassa education, that is there for producing fundamentalists is not stopped, if steps are not taken for education and self-reliance of women, if women are not empowered at all levels, the fatwa-happy men will carry on their deeds in uninterrupted peace. If the rights and independence of women have to be established, if human rights and humanity are to triumph, then the use of religion must be stopped. If religion is treated with indulgence, fundamentalism too will get a free run.

I said that those issuing the fatwa must be punished. Nilofar said there was no sense in paying them the slightest heed. Her voice was replete with self-confidence. Nilofar had believed that the tiny fundamentalist force would be defeated; she would win this war. There was no reason why she should not win because she had committed no offence. After safely concluding a parachute jump, she had customarily hugged her instructor. This happened not many days ago. Nilofar had never imagined that the fundamentalists would be paid heed to and that she would not be rendered the slightest regard. Faced with constant threats and receiving no support from either the government or the people, Nilofar was finally forced to tender her resignation. Or, maybe, pressure from the party and the government compelled her to resign. Who suffered defeat? The fundamentalists? Or Nilofar? Nilofar. She was punished even though she had done no wrong. Nilofar had thought that being a minister she had enormous power. But she had forgotten that she was a woman and that women were powerless. She had forgotten that in a crowd of patriarchal males, she was nothing at all, nothing at all. She possessed only that much power as had been given to her by the powerful men. Men could take back that power any moment at one snap of the fingers. Nilofar had forgotten that she was a woman; forgotten that in any war she would be compelled to accept defeat; forgotten that this was a man's world.

Women keep forgetting this, particularly women who have had a few opportunities and advantages, women who have risen above their class, women who have tasted official power. They forget that men can whisk them off from any height and at any moment.

Nilofar is not a minister any more. Illustrious posts like that of a king, a minister, *vazir*, judge, president and so on were made by men for men alone. By giving women the opportunity to ascend to these posts, some men try to prove that men and women enjoy equal rights. However, you need not keep your eyes and ears wide open, just opening a little will do, to understand that there is no equality at all.

We can well imagine how powerful the fundamentalist fatwa-issuers must be to be able to unseat Nilofar from power. We can but observe how despite being a minister, and despite having done no wrong, despite brimming with self-confidence and mental strength, Nilofar was easily unseated. Nilofar's offence lay not in touching a male other than her husband or even embracing him. Her offence lay in her being a woman. If she had not been a woman, no touch or embrace of hers would have been treated as an offence. She had to suffer because she was born a woman, not because she embraced anybody. If she had not been a woman, she could have hugged 10 million paratroopers with ease; nobody would have bothered to issue a fatwa. Neither would she have had to resign from the ministry.

We are witnessing things like this for many many years. Can we do anything about it except recording our protest? No one cares a fig for our protests. People with a conscience and intellect have been protesting against patriarchy for a thousand years. What good has it done? Has patriarchy suffered the slightest crack? Some weak people have spewed venom against patriarchy in all societies across all ages. The powerful have not. If they had, then girls the world over would not have had to suffer from the crime of being girls.

Those who consider that religion may coexist with women's independence either do not know what religion means or are ignorant of what women's independence means. Many indulge in fantasy that despite patriarchy, despite a male-dominated society, despite power resting in the hands of men, women's independence will flourish. Nilofar too had believed in such an idea, and now she has realized well how grossly she had miscalculated. She has said, "Believe me, neither of us intended to hurt our culture or society." She has argued there was nothing treasonable or anti-Islamic in jumping from an airplane in a parachute. True, it is not treason, but indeed an anti-Islamic act. Which Islamic text says that woman can travel on land, in water, in the air without a guardian? Women are not supposed to step out of their doors, and even if they do, they should be draped in a *burqa* from head to toe. Women are forbidden to exhibit their physical beauty in front of non-husband males. Women not abiding by this prohibition imposed by Allah are acting against the religion. Nilofar is guilty in the eyes of many, but not guilty in the eyes of any sane person.

Since the strong and the weak, the rich and the poor, the powerful and the powerless are conspicuously and vehemently present in this world, perhaps, it is natural that the meek will be oppressed. This has been taken for granted. When a meek man is oppressed, those engaged in class struggle or those fighting for human rights come forward to stand in support of the oppressed man. But when a woman is oppressed, not so many people, so many parties or so many organizations come forward. People are used to witnessing women being oppressed right from their birth. No one will be particularly hurt because Nilofar has lost her berth in the ministry. That a woman actually got a ministerial post, a post meant for men, is itself cause for surprise. Nilofar is now a woman who has climbed down from a man's post, a woman ready to accept humbly all punishments meted out to her for being guilty of being a woman. Nilofar is now any Sufiya or Shefali, any Swapna or Swati. One of those women after whom the media will not run, about whom the media will not enquire even if they strain under want and disease, will not give a second look even if their husbands thrash them every night; nobody will save them from the ceaseless torture and oppression. Only if they are raped, or happen to die an accidental death, will the news spread far and wide. Everybody will jump on the bandwagon. A woman who has been raped, or a woman who has died an unnatural death, both make for sexy news. In this society, women are recognized as sexual items. News on rape causes rapist men to be secretly aroused. News of death, especially when a man has gruesomely murdered a woman, is given prominence. The hair-raising account of how a woman has been hacked and burnt to death is perhaps an educative and entertaining experience for many men.

If no woman ever forgets that she is a woman, if no woman ever forgets that everything—from religion to the only armour she has at her disposal to don during times of danger—is anti-women, only then perhaps women will be able to step forward in the right direction. Only then will she refrain from proudly adorning, courtesy the charity of man, the posts created by men. Instead she will strive, even risking her life in the process, for converting those posts into posts for women. This struggle is a difficult one. What can be more difficult than fighting against religion and patriarchy—the two enormous powers of the world! Confronting every woman today are two ferocious giants; either fight them or die. Woman die even if they compromise, they die if they fight. When death is the inevitable, is it not better to die after having clawed and bitten at your enemy?

***

19

Biting and Scratching in the Name of Love

In a society where men are the masters, the controller of women, there can be no courtship in the true sense of the term between a man and a woman. A man, who grows up with the best facilities, can at best flirt with a half-fed, least-cared woman, but can never love her. Our society looks upon man's compassion for woman and woman's respect for man as love. This kind of love drags her body and soul into an unequal relationship. What a man does with a woman's heart is an open secret. But what does he do with her body? As he has no respect for her, it is quite obvious that he has no regard for her body as well. His enjoying her body can be compared to a tiger's enjoyment with a deer. The tiger that has no feelings for the deer mercilessly tears its entrails before consuming it. It feels hungry, it hunts the deer and it consumes its prey. Satiating its hunger, it will go back to its own territory. Next time, when hungry again, it will pounce upon another deer and if it does not get one, it will kill a buffalo or a human as substitute.

When a man bites a woman's lips, as though he is crushing a bean, they call it a kiss. The woman who experiences the taste of a kiss in this manner accepts it that kiss means a bite on her lips with sharp teeth, kiss means swollen lips, torn and ragged lips and bleeding lips. Next to lips, the men fall for the female breasts. They press and smash and crush her bosom to pulp. They scratch her with all their nails to tear her breasts. Had they loved a woman they would have demonstrated their love for her body as well. His fingers would have been softer and tender and claws and teeth would have rolled back. The man is obsessed with his own pleasure only. He is least bothered about his female partner's likes and dislikes. He has never tried to understand her mind. Even if he happens to know, he feels no urge to satisfy her.

Women also do not know what will make them really happy. How can they? They believe what the men make them believe. A woman has no independent thoughts and feelings. In sex, he is the master, megalomaniac, macho, and she's his toy. He is superior, she is inferior. He is active, she is passive. If she were not passive, he would have faced a tougher situation. If the deer resists, the tiger will have to work harder. Men are all in all in society—in the household affairs, education, health, culture and where not. They are terribly active to shape the policies in terms of patriarchy. So how can he allow a woman, the toy of his pleasure, to be active in the bed? Never. He will not light fire in the house of his own ego. He will allow the woman to move so much as it is necessary for his own delightful sensation.

Vatsayana has clearly spoken about 64 erotic postures, yet the Bengali man is content with one posture—the missionary variety. He is least bothered to spend time for the rest of the 63 postures. He has only mastered the skill of keeping his female partners as passive as vegetables.

Males have a low level of sense of humour. That's why they are worried about a woman's sense of wit and humour. He has little time and energy to indulge in foreplay, though he knows without it the erotic journey will never be smooth. He is ready, so everyone must be prepared. The horse is ready so must be the reins. Order! Order! Women must receive the aroused man instantly. Otherwise, how can you be a real woman? How can you identify yourself with the waitress? How can you be called giver of pleasure and expert in entertainment? Women are ever prepared to sacrifice everything for the sake of man's joys and delights.

How many women do know what orgasm is? She knows everything is for her man's pleasure only. It is not that she will not have pleasure; her pleasure centres around her capacity to ensure man's pleasure. Other than this, no pleasure is allotted for her. For ages, men have inculcated in women the motto of self-abnegation. Without regret, she will renounce her independence, her separate identity, her will, her happiness, and he will relish this resignation of a woman. There is nothing more tasty and delicious than this.

Had women been homosexual, they would have been much happier. The disadvantages of heterosexual women are that they have to spend their lives by accepting slight, neglect, humiliation and dissatisfaction. The man is supposed to play his fingers as softly as possible to help the woman blossom bit by bit like a bud. Then she will stare with eyes burning with lust like a tigress, and not like a bayed deer. The man's breath, his touch, his body odour, his sweat, his sex desires will arouse in her intensely erotic passion. But does it happen at all? In reality, he rises like a monster determined to rape a woman. It is nothing but megalomania or machismo. The masculine pleasure is to smash and crush and squeeze a woman into pulp.

The world belongs to men. India belongs more to men than in other countries. Men wish to get women's company as and when they have an arousal with utter disregard to their consent. Women should have no desire of their own. If they have at all they should be reticent about it. Her body should not experience an arousal; she should do everything to lull her arousals into sleep. She is forbidden to approach him first for sex. She is forbidden to kiss him. She should never take aggressive role during intercourse. She is not the master of it, she is a slave. During the coitus, if she reciprocates instead of remaining passive, he gets the greatest shock resulting in the drooping of the penis. His erection is in a state of uncertainty unless she plays the role of a passive sex slave.

If a woman moans in sexual hunger, she is branded as a sex maniac. If a man hungers for sex, he is honoured for his potency. With such discrimination existing in a society, can anyone expect a healthy relationship between a man and a woman? Never! When two people are engaged in sex, it is described in colloquial Bengali as 'he is doing with her,' instead of 'they are doing it. The very language is the indication of a terrible gender discrimination.

The world is full of impotents, though outwardly, it is not possible to identify them. None of the impotents seem to have any sense of shame, disgrace. Though they have no erection, their heads are held high! The women who are the victims of those impotent partners spend their days in shame and nightmares. The impotents have no concern for the sexual pleasure of women. Had they been worried about their impotence, and concerned about the pleasure of women, they would have tried to rectify themselves. They would not have tortured women in the name of sex.

The day men will repose faith in the equal rights of men and women, the day men will unconditionally honour women's liberty, the day men will throw away their vile masculinity, the day men will give up their brutality, the day men will become human beings and enfold women with actual love and admiration and honour, that day men and women shall enjoy the actual bliss of love and sex. Before that the situation is like one enjoys and the other suffers.

Women's liberty means sexual liberty—many comment sarcastically. But it is a fact. Without sexual freedom, women can never acquire real freedom. Never! If a woman has no freedom over her body, she can never be free in any sense. In spite of her education or economic independence, she cannot be emancipated from the status of sex-slave. When they will enjoy freedom of sex, liberating themselves from this abominable status, only then I will call them independent. By sexual freedom

I don't mean that she will lie in the bed with every Tom, Dick and Harry. The right to say no is also an essential aspect of this freedom. She is flanked with rapists all around. Her right to say no to the call of the impotent and rapist is essential for her freedom. She must have the right to knockout those men who want to make a show of their manliness by biting her lips and scratching her nipples. She should acquire the freedom of sex by discarding men who are obsessed with their own pleasure, who are least bothered about the pleasure of women.

***

20
Listen, Golden Women
of a Golden Bangla

Two women political leaders have been ruling Bangladesh
for many years now—Hasina and Khaleda. Khaleda is
undoubtedly a friend of religious fundamentalism. Hasina used
to be regarded as secular, representing a force that has pitted itself
against fundamentalism. Many had thought that Hasina's Awami
League would win the elections because the power exercised by the
religious fundamentalists and the terror unleashed by them have
made the lives of the people miserable. It was hoped that Hasina
was the only leader who could stand up to the fundamentalists
and bring back secularism to the country, stop the proliferation
of madrassa education, put an end to the issuance of fatwas by
the clerics and curb the sway of the fundamentalists. As the
country was being destroyed by the reactionary fundamentalist
forces, well-wishers of the country quite naturally turned to
Hasina. But Hasina stunned and shocked everyone by declaring

that she would give the fatwa-ists the right to issue fatwas. She further said that she would give madrassas the status of colleges and universities, promulgate the blasphemy law and would not rest before turning the people's republic of Bangladesh into a purely Islamic state. Habibur Rehman, who in 1993 announced a fatwa against me and fixed the price of my head, is a candidate of Awami League in the next election. Hasina has unhesitatingly extended the hand of friendship to the leader of the Islamic fundamentalist party, Shaikhul Hadis, a man who has no equal when it comes to unleashing terror throughout the country. Isn't it unbelievable! Though unbelievable, it is all absolutely true. Though unbelievable it is nevertheless true that there is no possibility the country called Bangladesh can ever return to its principles of democracy, socialism and secularism.

People knew Awami League as a progressive and secular party. But now is there any difference between Awami League and a fundamentalist party? To tell the truth, when it comes to principle and ideology, there is no real difference among parties like Jamaat-e-Islami, Islamic Unity coalition (Islami Oikya Jot), BNP and Awami League. So what can the country's future be like at this moment! I am incapable of dreaming of any prospect about this country. The country has turned into a den of Muslim extremist terrorists. And the rest of the lot, who claim they are not extremists, that they are against fundamentalism, are secretly compromising with fundamentalism. Many people will vehemently deny that religion is the root of fundamentalism. And it is because they believe in religion that today even secular people cannot put up a sufficiently strong fight against fundamentalism.

Fundamentalism did not drop from the sky. Fundamentalism arose out of religion. Allah or Ishwar or God—they are all fundamentalists, and so are their devotees. Religious gurus and godmen are all undoubtedly fundamentalists. Fundamentalists are those who not only believe in the fundamental principles of religion, but also wish countless people to do the same. Those in Bangladesh who claim that they are not fundamentalists, do they not believe in the fundamental principle of religion? Many of them secretly believe in it. And most of those who don't, dare not declare that openly.

Bangladesh was the land of Sufi saints. In my childhood, I have seen very old men, who had nothing better to do, hop on their sticks to the mosque, not so much to read the *namaz* as to gossip with other elderly men. There would be some 10 or 12 people in the mosque in all. And now? The mosque is overcrowded with young people. They block the roads to read the *namaz*. What a picture of Bangladesh I behold! Who created this madness over religion? I blame the politicians. I blame the rich Arab countries which have almost bought the poor countries in order to propagate their religion. I blame the anti-socialist, capitalist neo-cons. Bangladesh is no more a golden Bangla. Was it ever! There was just a possibility of making it so in '52, '69 and '71. But all that endless possibility has disappeared in these few years.

The country is awash in religious bigotry. Political leaders are turning into fundamentalists and competing with each other to prove who is the most religious and the greatest fundamentalist. Has anyone thought what this will do to the country? Politicians will of course enjoy the comfort of power for a few days. But who will soon be engulfed in misfortune? Everyone knows it will be the girls, who have to suffer all their lives due to religion. To bring in religion within the fold of the state, society, the law and the family is to welcome violence against women, discrimination between man and woman, child marriage for girls, polygamy for men, the law of stoning women to death for supposedly committing adultery, beating women to death for not wearing the *burqa* or being disobedient to the husband, the horror of triple *talaq*, and imprisonment, unemployment, illiteracy, ill health, slavery and suffering for women.

The snake called fundamentalism has its hood raised to lunge at women. Today, I am struck speechless with anxiety for women of my motherland, a Bangladesh swarming with poisonous snakes. It is said that the anti-fundamentalist forces will protest when pushed against the wall. But will men protest? Will men really protest? It is men whom religion provides with all kinds of comfort. Masters known as men wring out every bit of comfort and luxury possible by riding roughshod over women, trampling them under their feet and crushing them collectively. Neither religion nor fundamentalism ever causes men to suffer. It is women who suffer from both. If anybody is pushed against the wall, it will be women. In fact, they should have had their backs to the wall a long time back. It is a mystery why they still haven't. Or maybe, their backs are indeed against the wall, but they have been made so insensitive that they cannot feel it. The brains of girls have become so dull that they do not understand that all men are the same, be they fundamentalists or something else. They will all make women suffer. They will all kick at women, they will all punch at women. They will dump the rights of women into the gutter. They will gangrape the freedom of women and murder it in cold blood. Fundamentalist or not, all men have done it and will do it. They have done it in the past, they are doing it now, and they will continue to do it in the future. They will do it till the day men are trampled to death. Till the day their pride is pulverized. Till their masculinity is ripped into pieces and negligently thrown into a stinking ditch.

Hasina is a woman. Everybody will now argue that she is a woman. True, but she is a representative of men. She is an accomplice of fundamentalism, an accomplice of religion. An accomplice of patriarchy. There is not a single 'man' like Hasina in Bangladesh. I know that women are the carriers and bearers of patriarchy. But I never knew so sharply that any woman could become such an atrocious and outrageous anti-woman 'man'.

Many women do harm to other women. They do so unknowingly. But Hasina, I know, is consciously and knowingly doing such harm to women. She knows fully well that once at the peak of power, the fundamentalists will first of all bring disaster in the lives of women. Despite knowing fully well that women will be swallowed up by the raging fire of *Shari'ah* laws, the flames of fatwas and the barbarism of religious laws, she made this terrible decision. Many will interpret this decision of Hasina's as tactics. But I say this is tantamount to playing with fire. It cannot have happy consequences. It will never have happy consequences.

Wherever I look today, I see such moral corruption of women. Isn't giving up one's rights for the pleasure of men, being servants to men, being representatives of men, synonymous with the moral corruption of women? Nothing else can make women more depraved. Let no woman emulate Hasina's depravity. Let all women together cry shame on a debauch like Hasina. Let all women have the courage, power and honesty to cry 'shame'.

***

21
Let Girls be Boys

As a child, like most other girls, I too craved to change myself into a boy. Suddenly waking up in the morning, I would see myself as a boy! I would then get the love and attention of my parents. I would get whatever I wished for. I would want the most expensive toys and I would get them. I would get fashionable clothes and shoes, and, even better, the best of the food available in the house. I would be able to go wherever I wanted to. I would play in the largest playground in the city. No one would stop me from doing anything. There would be a hundred and one aides waiting to deliver all my desires. I am the king, the emperor, a son, the world; I am God.

As I grew older, my sufferings increased. I was scolded and sworn at because I was a girl. Someone would yank my hair at the pettiest excuse. Huddling in a corner of a room, I would shed tears and muse over why could not I become a boy. Men would cast a lusty look at my breasts, grabbed them whenever they got a chance. When I began menstruating, they told me I was polluted—I was barred from doing this or that, from touching certain things. I lived in the fear of being pounced upon, being raped or strangled to death. Someone, anyone, might throw acid on my face, or burn me after pouring kerosene all over my body.

How secured I could have been if I could turn into a boy. I could live a life without fear. Could have lived comfortably. Would have got all the cooperation of the family, society, the law and the state. Could have concentrated on my studies, research, achievements, income and my living. But only because I was a girl, I had to be busy about my protection all the time. Even at work, I had to protect myself from innumerable predators. I could never walk about alone, carefree, on the streets, in the parks, sit on the banks of a river or stand for a while taking in the sea.

It is a man's world. Nothing in this world, no one, no creature is as insecure as a woman. Without a companion, I was never secure in the cities, in the ports, the villages, the towns, in the fields... nowhere. I had, always, to take guards with me for my protection. Left alone, I am not enough to protect myself. So, someone had to be with me. The state and its laws, society and its mores, nothing is adequate for the security of any girl. Some people might retort that there is little security for men either. I agree, the lack of security threatens men as well. Nevertheless, in comparison with what men face, the inadequacy of security faced by women is a million times more, only because women were born as women. Men do not face this. No one else in the animal world faces this.

This society teaches both men and women right from their childhood that the male is a little more human than the female. Women are physically and mentally weak. They are not fit to do a lot of things. They should not say, demand or even think of certain things. They cannot be aggressive. You are weak, physically and mentally. You are not fit for liberty. Repeatedly indoctrinated with such teaching, the self-confidence of women gets crushed. They do not unite, protest, oppose. They do not throw kicks. Women not only remain silent against this anti-female society, there are women who actually hold it in high esteem and celebrate it.

Men think the discrimination that exists between men and women is solely women's problem, not theirs, and therefore, it is the responsibility of women alone to launch movements against this subversion. They wonder about like irresponsible folks. But if a man seeks even minimal social welfare, he should come forward to bear the responsibility to help end gender disparity. A society is not healthy—and the question of calling it decent doesn't even arise—if the tradition of torturing one human being by another continues. Why should the responsibility of making society healthy be vested with women only, and not with men as well? Society belongs to both men and women! Does it mean men do not want equality and equal rights? If they had desired so, why the powerful men at the helm are not rooting out this disparity in one blow?

They are not interested, for had they done so, they would have deprived themselves from the opportunity of sexually harassing women. Indian society brags so much about family; but contemptible crimes are committed inside the family. Sexual molestation of infant girls continues unabated. A small girl child is not safe in the family of her own father, uncles, elder brothers and grandfathers.

A recent report by the central government has revealed that 53 per cent of Indian children, somehow or the other, are victims of sexual abuse. It includes rape, anal sex, sexual torture and forcible kissing. One-fifth of children become victims of severe sexual abuse. In 83 per cent of the cases, people close to the family commit the abuse, and in 50 per cent cases, the offender is known to the girl. The whole thing is hushed up. No one speaks against it. The children remain in helpless obscurity. In 70 per cent of the cases, they cannot reveal anything.

West Bengal is at the top of the crime table. However, we hear all the time from both men and women that this state is the most progressive one, women might be harassed in other states, but never in West Bengal. The word 'progressive' is used very widely in the case of West Bengal. We do not know what their reaction will be now after going through the Centre's scrutiny in this report. They might say with a sneer that if it is so, then it must be in the rural areas and not in the cities. If told of an instance at Bagbazar, they may say at least it is in the north and not in the south Kolkata! If an instance in Tollygunge in the south is cited, they will say: Let it happen in Tollygunge but it will not happen in Ballygunge. I have rarely seen such indifferent people. When the house of a neighbour is burning, they will remain quiet till the time their own tails catch fire.

Little girls feel so insecure because of such sexual abuses that 48.4 per cent of them are now asking why they were not born boys instead. Like me, they too wish to turn themselves into boys. It will free them from endless torments. A woman suffers not in her girlhood, but all through her life. They are liberated only at death.

I dream of a day when all women in the world will be changed into men and no such thing as woman will exist any more. May be, only then will there be no such thing as 'masculine'. The male-dominated society wants to grind women. If no woman is around, whom they will grind? They will fight among themselves and get killed. However, some among them will again ask for peace. They will start a movement for class struggle and equality. Men will become homosexuals and will pray to their God for the womb that at some auspicious moment would bear a girl child. Men will then dream how, after the birth of that girl, all men in the world will be raping her each moment as long she is alive. When that girl gives birth to another girl child, men will be raping her too. But this masculine dream will never come true. Men will keep seeing this dream, till the time they die one after the other... and thus human existence will come to an end.

After all, why should women have to survive tolerating the injustices done to them by men just to save the human race? For what should women bear this responsibility? Extinction is better than that. Let only those animals live on this planet who live in equality, love and happiness and those who do not devour others or do not kill others savagely. Let mankind become history - the history of men's scandals.

***

22

Adultery goes up as Divorces do not take Place

Divorces do not take place in this country. There is no reason for divorce. When a man and a woman get married, there remains a written or unwritten clause that the husband will earn money, will take the responsibility of living, and the wife will obey his orders, will be a partner in the bed, will look after the family members and the household works, will produce children and will rear them. This is a contract. It is there in a love-marriage and also in a non-love arranged marriage. Thus, a man gets another one for their comfort and use. The wife is a human being, but without any brains, without any claim to her personal life. She should deprive herself from her birth rights and should dedicate herself to the service and comfort of her husband. Why should men forsake such slaves by divorcing them? If one does not want to bed with his wife, he may go for another. No one objects. Rather it is a precondition of being modern. A man has no need to divorce his wife. Why should there be any urge to change the slave? A slave is a slave. It will suffice if she has admiration for the master or the man. Why should one change the old one who has become apt in household work by virtue of her experience? So the men find no merit in change, and show no interest in doing that. They can take recourse to adultery if they do not feel attracted towards the wives, and even then the family runs perfectly. So, are they idiots to seek divorce? Why women accept their husbands' adultery? That is the question. The answer is: they are compelled to do so. What is the guarantee that other men will not do the same? Some say, adultery is in the blood of men. I say, not in blood, but in every nook and corner of patriarchy.

Live with whom you love. Where the minds join, join the bodies there, for the bird called mind lives in the body. Live with that person whom you have given your mind and your body. If such honesty was in everyone, the number of divorce would have increased. Both sides would not have lingered with a loveless relationship. If women were more independent, more conscious, then the number of divorce should have gone up. As the reason for not taking recourse to divorce is different for a man and a woman, so adultery is on the rise. It is bound to be so. The society will be swept by unhappy couples and sick adulterers. Many people consider the word adultery as conservative. I am not one of them. Any relationship calls for faithfulness. If love dominates the relationship, there will be faithfulness. Otherwise, it cannot be ensured by enacting laws. Continuation of a loveless relation not only pains the adults, but also the children. They watch daily violence, hatred, envy. Thereafter, can they grow up as healthy, beautiful, liberal and rational human beings? Impossible. Even if we are concerned about the future of the nation, we have to rescue the children from such environment. Breaking of loveless and intolerable relationships enduring in families after families is in the interest of the couples, the children, a healthy society and all. If it does not break, how something new will emerge? Can we dream of the beautiful while clinging on to the old and rotten?

We know why the husbands are not divorcing their wives. But why the wives are not doing so? The wives are watching their husbands' adultery, treachery, and double-standards; but are not divorcing them. There is no love, but they are living under one roof, or are being compelled to do so. Men often allege that their wives are no more attractive to them. The more the woman is working hard, giving birth to children, providing service and sacrificing her health, the more she becomes uninteresting to him. He goes for acquiring honey from some other flowers. His wife has turned uncouth, stale. The women can think in the same line too. They have more reasons to do so. In this society younger women are married with older women. In comparison to the wife, the husband seems an old haggard. A wife may feel that her husband is ugly, blindly self-seeker, greedy, rotten. Women surely feel so. At least, secretly. But why women do not leave these stale men and love some handsome younger men? Why they do not get involved in sex-game with such persons? Because, they do not have time. They bear the burden of household and the children. Even if that is taken care of, where will they go? The new man will also be another adulterer. Surely. That is why the women try to hide the adultery of their husbands by making the vermilion at the parting brighter and wearing bangles. They have no option. But, is it really so?

Adulterer is a word that has so long being used on women, instead of the men. Women have received punishment for that. Helpless women were compelled to have sex with those men who threatened them, enticed them, and tricked them to enter into such relation. Those women earned bad names. Called adulteress, and were punished. Now a new law is coming up as a result of insistence by the Women Commission to ensure that only men will be punished for adultery, and not women.

Just like the new law to prevent atrocities on women, this law on adultery is also a civilized one. The Gods have played enough with women. Indian men have been influenced so much by it that they too have turned experts in it. Now the adulterer will be punished for adultery. The one who deserves punishment will be punished. The inheritors of the gods had enough leeway so long. No more they will have it.

I feel sorry for women. They are fired upon, and then are hanged for receiving bullets. They die again and again after dying once. Who else dies so many times, hundreds of times, like women? I welcome the new laws, whether they will be implemented or not, sitting in a fearsomely anti-woman society. Let no more women be victims of the lies, tricks, dominance, conspiracies, wickedness, different standards, injustice, and adultery. Let women be salvaged from barbarism of men.

***

23

Why are Girls not Divorcing their Tyrannical, Adulterous Husbands?

The number of divorces is much less in India than in any other country of the world—only 11 for every 1,000 couples, says the study. In Russia, the rate of divorce is 65 per cent; in Sweden, 64 per cent; in Belgium, 56 per cent; in the United Kingdom, 53 per cent; in the United States 50 per cent; and in India, only 1.1 per cent. Ironically, the number of divorces is more in civilized nations where women are educated, conscious and self-reliant. This fact has been proved time and again. Surveys in the West have revealed that the rate of divorce is 50 per cent for first-time marriages and 60 per cent in case of re-marriages. The question is why are there so few divorces in India? The answer is very simple. Here, patriarchy holds much greater sway. Here even when women are allowed to acquire education, they are not allowed to become conscious or self-reliant; even if they are allowed to become self-reliant, they are not allowed liberty. But who will give women that which is theirs? Who is

the master who will give them their due? This is a question that
may well arise. The answer to this is simple. The master is man,
the anti-woman patriarchal society. Man and his system provide
for a woman's liberty only when they want to. Women's liberty
does not rest with women; it rests in the pockets of men's shirts,
or in the palm of their hands.

India is the country of those unfortunate women who have
far less power to divorce than in any other part of the world.
In this vast country—where there are people from so many
different religions and cultures, people of different views and
paths, people of so many different colours and manners, people
having immense wealth and living in crushing poverty—riots
and disturbances are only too common. There is malice, violence,
hatred and conflict all around. Misgiving and distrust lurk in the
mind. The discrimination between man and woman is as wide
as the sky and the earth. Even then, with the land so fertile for
divorce, why aren't divorces being produced! Many people claim
that women live in the land of plenty. But does that education,
which women acquire from academics, contain any lesson on
the equal rights of women and men? Is there data about the
fact that women do not get what they are entitled to, that is,
dignity by virtue of being human beings, by virtue of having
a separate identity? No, there isn't. Where is the consciousness
in women? Women are not conscious of the fact that they are
tortured and trampled, and denied their own rights, that women
should not put up with such oppression, that they ought to live
with their heads held high, that they should not falter thinking
that people might slander them, that if anybody stands in
their way they should kick him aside. How many women have

such consciousness? Women are becoming self-reliant, but is economic self-reliance giving them any confidence at all? Do they acquire the enabling quality to make decisions on their own? Is self-reliance in women providing them the grit to live alone? If self-reliance is aimed at handing all the money the women earn to their husbands and thereby get some prestige at their in-laws', then it is actually another name for dependence.

Most women in India do not know the meaning of independence. They think women's liberty means to smoke and drink, to wear skimpy dresses, dance at Tantra or Mantra or whatever discotheque, and sleep with a variety of men. Very few people are able to comprehend that this is not what liberty means, not at all. How many people understand that all those things—dancing or sleeping—is performed within the confines of the severest patriarchy, as commodities used by men, as objects of male pleasure? It should be understood that a woman can enjoy liberty even if she does not smoke and drink, or wear skimpy clothes, or dance at discotheques, or sleep around. Today, women do not have the ability to think in an independent way. Centuries of living in a patriarchal system has made them dull. Nothing in a woman is as desirable to men as is a dull brain. Just as a woman tucks a rose in the bun on her head, so has man tucked it in her head that liberty is a bad thing. She gets or looks for only that much liberty as men will give or wish to give them. Not only a woman's possessions and properties remain in the custody of man, her liberty too remains in his custody, just like a spool and kite. The spool is in man's hand. If he unwinds the string, the kite, or the woman, will fly; if he winds it up, the kite, or the woman, will crash to the ground. It is the man who will decide what length of string he will unwind, and what expanse of sky the woman will fly in, if at all. Does a woman know how to snatch the spool from man? Does anybody teach her that? Women, subjugated for thousands of years, do not know how to enjoy liberty. They do not even know the correct definition of liberty. If they had known the definition, the number of divorces would have shot up.

Among all the countries of the world, it is in India that the rate of divorce is so shamelessly low. Nowhere else is this as low. In other countries, there are 16 valid reasons for getting a divorce. In India, there are primarily five reasons. Since there is no uniform civil code in the country, the law is different for different religious communities. A Christian may not get a divorce for the same reason as a Hindu. A Hindu can seek divorce on the following grounds: adultery, disappearance, cruelty, sexual impotence, and prolonged physical and mental illness, sexual disease.

Although both women and men are capable of committing adultery, it is men who indulge in it. Men naturally do not allow women the kind of opportunities that they have reserved for themselves for committing adultery. A woman is a victim of man's adultery, yet, the victim is vilified as adulteress. It is the husband who commits adultery or indulges in sexual relations outside marriage; the wife meekly accepts it with head bowed down. Maybe her head is rather blunt.

Divorce can be sought if there has been no cohabitation for three years. But do wives divorce any husband on such a ground? A woman tire herself out trying to trace her husband who has disappeared; then she picks the good-for-nothing up from some gutter and welcomes him home with a lot of ceremony.

Husbands beat up their wives to pulp, yet women cannot give up the habit of looking up at them as god. Women are incessantly tortured both physically and mentally, yet, these cowards are unwilling to sever relationship with the brutes.

Sexual impotence is intrinsically associated with men. Yet, millions of girls spend years and years, ages and ages with impotent husbands without a murmur of protest. Women have been taught that sexuality or the pleasure derived from it is a man's affair, and that they should be content producing and rearing children. A cruel and ruthless patriarchy has not left a single means for women to know, learn and understand the truth, no way that their blunt heads can ever be sharpened.

Women spend ages, their entire life, with husbands suffering from sexual diseases, or with infirm, incapacitated, disabled husbands. They tend their husbands like a maidservant, and it is this role that patriarchy extols as loving sacrifice. This leaves our women pleased as punch.

Loveless cohabitation, discontent and hatred are witnessed in almost every house. Adultery and autocracy are rampant. In almost every house, women are shamelessly oppressed. Even then, women do not have the courage to stand on their feet with spine erect and head held high. They do not have the courage to build a shelter of their own. Women are given a detailed list of what might happen to them if they opt for divorce – for instance, men will make a grab for a divorcee woman, considering her to be one easily available. But who does not know that a woman need not be a divorcee for men to make a grab for her! Virgin or not, divorcee or otherwise, young or old, male hands or organs can reach out for any woman. They do not even leave a two-and-a-half-year-old kid. It is said that divorce leads to fall in a woman's economic condition. Well, so be it. So what if her economic condition deteriorates, she can at least live life on her own terms! If this is what thousands of women want today, if they respect their own wishes, if they live in one hundred per cent liberty and with one hundred per cent rights, then no tradition, prejudice or familial system will remain strong enough to hurl abuses at them or stand in their way. People speak of security. Is one's husband any real security? In every other house, wives are killed by husbands, doused in kerosene and set ablaze, strangled to death and then hung from the ceiling fan, raped every night. Is this what is called security? Statistics reveal that girls are tortured most at their husbands' house.

It is evident from the divorce rates that the condition of girls in India is very pathetic, that they are prisoners of domesticity, that they do not have the slightest right to enjoy their own rights. There is something called evolution, it goes on in the world. India is the only country in the world where there is no evolution in the status of women. Today, in the 21st Century, the so-called educated, conscious, self-reliant girls do not opt for divorce for the same reason that our grandmothers or their grandmothers—crazy with torture and caught in a loveless relationship—did not divorce their husbands.

***

24

Women Responsible for Making Men Inhuman?

At that point of time, media was carrying the news that Aishwarya Rai may get married to Abhishek, son of the megastar of Indian film Amitabh Bachchan. But the beloved megastar announced that his son would not marry her as their astrologer had predicted that in Abhishek's life Aishwarya would be ominous for him. They performed various pujas to stem the crisis. Thus, Aishwarya became fit to marry Abhishek. She too is a famous film-star. Now everybody started asking whether Aishwarya would be allowed to act even after her marriage? Would her in-laws allow her to continue in the film line? Abhishek was heard saying, "If Aishwarya wants to continue, she will continue". Nobody asked whether Abhishek will be stopped from acting after marriage. No one asked Aishwarya whether she would allow Abhishek to continue acting in films.

Is anyone surprised by this? No. All these are very natural. But why? Why no one raises the question that why marriage changes the life of the girl entirely, but not of the boy?

Many feminists say that education and economic self-reliance enable a woman to live as fully-independent human being. Must be wrong. Otherwise, why should a famous actress, educated and immensely rich, have to sacrifice herself in the scaffold of her husband's wishes? Then is it true that problems are embedded with this very concept of husband and marital life! Women are still prisoners of this system, be they educated or uneducated, self-reliant or not. Serve your husband, obey him, produce children for your husband, rear the children—this is patriarchy, and all women of the world are its victims. Men have protected this filthy ugly system for ages. Nowadays, a mantra is being inculcated in the heads of women, that they should consider their husbands-children-family life more important than themselves. Earlier, there was no scope of education for women. There was no question of achieving self-reliance. Now there are schools and colleges for them, they are having degrees, but it does not help. After passing out, they either turn housewives, or else, they do some job, but after taking permission of the father or the husband or the son. They are all tied with a strong rope. Men have made all arrangements so that women do not dare to free themselves. Men pull these ropes and that sway the heavy life and insecure future of women.

Gloria Steinem, the famous feminist writer, said, "I have yet to hear a man ask for advice on how to combine marriage and career."

Gloria made different comments on marriage. She said that once someone asked her why men gamble much more than women. She answered from common sense that women do not have much money. Then she said it was right, but incomplete answer. "In fact women's total instinct for gambling is satisfied by marriage." What about the other quote? "A liberated woman is one who has sex before marriage and a job after." On marriage, she also said, "Marriage works best for men than women. The two happiest groups are married men and unmarried women." It was thought that the slogan that got immense popularity in the decade of 60s was coined by Gloria: "A woman without a man is like a fish without a bicycle." As a fish does not need a bicycle, so a woman does not need a man, but it is difficult for women prejudiced with tantra and mantra to understand this.

So many Madhuris, Nitu Singhs, Kajols, Shri Devis, Karishmas wilted untimely because they got married. For women, marriage is dangerous. Like a curse. The western feminists came to the conclusion at one point of time that discrimination between women and men would not go till we can obliterate marriage. They felt that the first duty of the feminists is to break the institution of marriage as it makes women slaves of men. Without obliteration of marriage, women cannot be liberated.

In the 60s and 70s, marriage was not popular among women of the West. But like bad times, marriage has staged a comeback. As the darkest clouds come back, conservatism has come back.

In India, half of the sky is ever clouded. Here, marriage was never extinct. Here women were and still are being sacrificed in the scaffold of marriage. In a society where women have no rights, no originality and independent existence, where they adopt the surnames of their husbands, where one marks herself as a property of someone else by using certain symbols and has to take shelter in someone else's house leaving her own, where the others decide a woman's future, there how marriage can be done away with!

Still now, economic self-reliance of women is not considered real self-reliance. The value that is attached to a man's earnings is not attached to a woman's earning.

Men earn for three reasons: for money, for status, and for satisfaction. The reasons are same for a woman, but the order is: first satisfaction, second status and third money. The upper class and even the middle class behave in a way as though women have no great need for money, and they do it for they feel like doing it, for satisfaction, for passing time.

It seems that only poor women need money as their husbands are vagabonds and wicked, as their husbands cannot earn much or give them much, as they have to feed themselves and their families. Middle class and upper class women are happy that they are not poor, that they can lead a comfortable life with what their husbands earn. They themselves are to be there only as show pieces in the house.

Women are still not waging a war against patriarchy for their liberation and self-reliance. Still, they are adding to their fall, even if they are rich, highly educated, or famous. These women blindfold them to claim that women have got their liberty in India. What they do not say is that in India a woman falls victim to sexual harassment every 26 minutes, is raped every 34 minutes, a woman is kidnapped every 43 minutes and a woman is killed every 93 minutes. This is the figure the government provides. It must be three times more if recorded by non-government teams.

Maximum number of women is killed inside their houses, by their husbands. All over the world women are exploited and tortured at home. No place is more unsafe for a woman than her husband's house. Here husbands are treated as gods. These gods decide whether they will allow the genius of their wives to radiate. Whatever be the extent of their genius, women will have to leave everything if their husbands do not want them to work outside. Even then there is a great urge among women to sacrifice their lives for the family that, in fact, tear them apart. Does this urge come from within? Or is it imposed on them?

I believe this is imposed on them. I believe that if women achieve a sense of dignity, they will revolt against patriarchy. They will live on their own. Men, their tantras and mantras, and the society they have built are scared of this. Has not the time come for men to be scared, to break down, to cry? For how long, women will make men inhuman by carrying them on their shoulders?

***

25

Do Men Deserve Women's Love?

I have but one fault. To fall in love. Whenever I am in love, I become very sincere to the man. I then forgive even the direst of his offences. I have rebuked myself for this many a times. I have often said to myself, "Do whatever you like, but never fall in love". But neither my heart nor my body abides by that. Since my heart is always open for anyone to walk in, handsome men can have entry anytime. At first sight, each one of these men gives me the impression that he does not believe in patriarchy and is miles away from superstition or orthodoxy of religion. He must be an exceptional lover. Love makes me sink into the oceans of imagination. In that submerged state of being, I imagine that man is respectful towards the female race; has hundred per cent faith in independence of women; is one who would himself fight for the rights of women. But as days pass, my consciousness begins to surface from its submerged state and in the end I get myself back. Breaking my trust, my love makes it explicit that like the others, he is also a misogynist, he also would never lose an opportunity to ruin a woman.

'Men do not deserve the love of women,' I believe, but still I fall in love with men. This is because though I tried, I could not become a homosexual, and I have a fierce lust for men. I get extreme pleasure in enjoying a handsome, well-built, slim, sharp-profiled male body. I am not fit to make myself a commodity for men. Do I instead like men to be a commodity? No. In this misogynist society, where at every door a woman is treated as a commodity by a man, it is impossible to take a man as a commodity. If it were possible I would have avenged at least once by turning them into commodities. But what I want I do not get here; equal rights. Men here do not know what equal rights mean. Those who have heard about equal rights have merely heard these words; they do not understand anything.

Men are, actually, all alike. There is hardly a difference between men from the East, or the West, or the South, or the North. Whatever difference exists is from the exterior. From inside, they are one and the same. Whether self-supporting or parasitic, whether from an upper class or a lower class, they are all alike. Once a man from a lower class followed me for a long time for little favours. How could I give him my favours? Rather, I showered my love on him. And as soon as I had done it, he began to take advantages. And then he nudged me and started asking me: "Hey, who are you? Who?" It's all the same to give a man love as to give him undue favour. They only know how to take love. They have never learnt how to give it. How would they learn? Who would teach that? After birth, they take their first lessons inside their homes where they notice different roles for their fathers and mothers. They see that their mothers are giving love, respect and service to their fathers; and their fathers, unconcerned and least worried, are enjoying everything. There is no end to such lessons. When men step out of the home, they get their second lesson and then the third.

A man is as much celebrated indoors as he is outside. He plays the role of a master. He is the overlord in matters of politics, economics and even social affairs. No man is ready to give up even the slightest of the benefits he is enjoying. This is the scenario in India. But even in the countries of the West, where women have acquired substantial authority, the situation is quite the same. I have seen that the white skin male lover too is mean, jealous, wicked and conceited. Actually, men by their race are extremely malicious towards women. Maybe its not proper to accuse racially. Men are made to be malicious towards women. For centuries, they have been taught that they know more, they understand better, they are physically stronger, intellectually superior and belong to a higher race. Therefore, it is very natural that men would ignore this ignorant, under-informed, weak, unintelligent women race. They would only use women to serve their ends.

I get angry on myself. I am otherwise an independent-minded, self-reliant, strong-willed and bold individual with my head always held high; but whenever I am in love, I become a weak, two-legged creature. When I fall in love, my intelligent self vanishes in a sudden gush of wind. Foolish and worthless, I lie within my lover's grasp. I become troubled by my fattening abdomen and get excessively worried about my double chin. I start disliking my nose, my eyes and my face. I cannot tolerate my grey hair; my hair-setting begins to appear disgusting. I begin to crave for Rekha's appearance and Sushmita Sen's figure. I do not like whatever is mine. I begin to look at myself through my lover's eyes, because then I lose my own capacity to see things. I generate a complex and with that complex I look at myself, every time. I look at myself almost a thousand times. The more I see myself, I become weaker. The more I look at myself, the more I try to impress him in various ways. My ignorance, my frustration and my helplessness begin to show. The fire of my love burns my self-confidence to ashes. I can no more identify myself. I am now a creature—meek, bent down and immovable. I desperately try to please my lover with my looks or delight him with my qualities. I do not have my own perception of anything anymore. My senses gradually become useless. There remains only the empty skull, with no brain inside. I start losing my own self. My originality, my pride, my firmness, my courage and strength are blown to pieces in the stormy currents of my love. The current becomes stronger; I become all the more a poor, degraded, decrepit. Conversely, my lover becomes more and more powerful. The more I bend down, the more delighted he becomes; the more he gets inflated by his male ego, the more he becomes a megalomaniac—an incredible hulk, more obsessed with self-importance.

Who has taught me that I have to impress my lover? Are these some old teachings lurking in my mind? These teachings are as dangerous as cancer: they are ruinous, they bring in destruction. They invite death to devour life entirely. And I, full of fierce life-force, striving against all religions and all fundamentalisms of the world, against the vile patriarchy, against war and bloodshed, I, who fight everywhere for the sake of humanity with the uncompromising self in me, ultimately surrender before the inhuman males. Before them, who enjoy the benefits of patriarchy, who enjoy at the cost of the trampled and oppressed female race.

What argument can I offer for this! For this mistake, for this degradation! The only consolation I have is that I get disillusioned as soon as I am lashed on my back. Whenever a man starts riding on my head, my head begins to reel. Under the circumstances, the only consolation I have is that I cannot rest in peace unless I get rid of him. I gain immense strength in my mind and body when it is time to drive a man down, to thrust aside a male like a spider. Breaking open the shackles of love, removing the dust and stains of my lover, I can again stand erect on my feet. The erect self in me does not compromise with any discrimination. The firm self in me does not look back. The steadfast self in me does not seek a man's favour. This unyielding individual can have love and friendship only with one species which is called human being. In this society, man is only a male, not yet a human being. And as long as he remains so, there is no question of any love.

Will men ever become human beings? Being immersed in the extreme form of patriarchy, they can become anything but human beings. By human being I understand an individual who has humanity in him, one who possesses humane qualities and one who believes in humanism. By human being, I understand someone who does not wrong other human beings, one who does not believe in inequality and one who does not have the gendered notion of himself as belonging to a superior race.

Only those human beings who do not accept even the slightest inequality between man and woman, who protest against inequality, who struggle against it and practice not even the least bit of this inequality in their own lives. To dishonour women, to ignore them for being women are the features rooted in a man's character. Will men like to lose their character? When the male being surfaces from within the lover, he no longer remains a lover. I have repeatedly observed this in my life. Time and again I have made the mistake of considering my lover not as a male, but as a human being.

The world would have been very beautiful if women like me, who believe in love, who suffer, who lay their lives for it, could raise their heads and stand erect throwing aside all dirt and filth of the male race, leading a life devoid of men. I swear by truth that no man deserves to get even the slightest of a woman's love unless he comes out of the patriarchy.

I do not believe in the concepts of caste, clan and community, etc. Those who divide people in different communities are communal. I revere men as men, irrespective of their gender, religion, caste, clan and community.

***

26

Homosexuals, Come Out
of your Closets

Almost half of my western friends are homosexuals.
Consequently, I am often seen in gay bars and discotheques
in Europe and America. I merrily join the huge Gay Pride Parade
held in New York every year as a gay-supporter. Homosexuals
have been fighting for their rights for many years now. They
have secured many rights, but there are also many rights that
are yet to be attained. Homosexuals enjoy maximum rights in
the countries of North Europe. There they are not only allowed
to marry, the question of right of succession of an adopted child
has also been settled. In those countries, homosexuals have come
up to be heads of states and prime ministers.

Those who do not support the rights of homosexuals fail to
support the cause of human rights. Every person has the right to
be sure of her/his sexual orientation, find a partner accordingly
and live together with her/him. Many of my homosexual friends
live together. One or two of them have opted to marry. They have

adopted children. The other day, on a visit to the cosy home of two lesbian friends of mine, I found that one of them had just become a mother. Strange! How did you get the sperm? Did you sleep with a man? No, she had not gone to bed with a man. They had got the sperm from a gay friend. My two lesbian friends were bringing up the newborn with equal care and affection. When a man and a woman are the parents of a child, it is the woman who has to take care of the child all by herself. How many men share the workload of bringing up a baby, like feeding her, putting her to sleep, changing her diapers and so on?

When both parents are women, not only does the child enjoy greater care, she also grows up in an atmosphere that is free from discrimination. The responsibility of bringing up the child is not imposed only on one of the partners. The most positive aspect in a family of two women is that there is no problem of macho superiority and sexual high-handedness.

The other day in Kolkata—this very Kolkata which is supposed to be a hugely progressive city and the cultural capital of India—a lesbian girl, cringing in shame, came up to me and recounted her agony. She has not married any man. Her parents are rather sore. The girl prefers the company of other girls. But she faces censure when she takes a girl to her room. The entire neighbourhood is seething with indignation. They say she is a bad woman. She wants to live together with her girlfriend, but finds it impossible in the city of Kolkata. The girl was crying as she narrated her story. I told her, let people say what they like, you go ahead with what you wish to do. I did say so, but I wondered how the girl would stay on in this city! They will not let her live. People are losing their jobs on the charge of being homosexuals. The girl turns blue in fear of losing her job, in fear of getting ousted from the locality. I feel very sorry for the girl, for the way she is suffering. I feel sorry for the conservative homophobics caught up in this rotten, old patriarchal system. I feel sorry for their idiocy.

When it is a curse to be born a girl, it is beyond comprehension of most people what it is to be a lesbian. There is a law against homosexuality. If you are caught, you will be sentenced to 10 years' imprisonment—yes, in this land of democracy Really unbelievable! How easily the right to express one's opinion as well as the entire gamut of human rights is violated in this democratic country! How many people protest?

According to official statistics, every hour one girl is raped in this country, every six hours a girl is burnt to death for being unable to pay dowry, and in 80 per cent of illegal abortions, the foetus is female. Yes, girls have the right to be raped, to be tortured, to die. But they do not have the right to love another girl. A girl must love a man, she must offer herself to a man, she must dedicate her life to a man. If you do not comply, you will not be given an inch of space in this patriarchal system.

A European lesbian friend of mine came to Kolkata two years ago. Working for an NGO, she toured not just the city but also distant villages for two months. I met her just before she was supposed to return to Europe. She told me what she had been up to. She said that she had had sexual relations with at least 12 girls. I was startled. Were they willing?

She replied, "Of course, they were willing."

"Were they married?"

"Yes, they were, though a few were unmarried."

"Not frigid?"

"Certainly not."

"Wasn't it very difficult to get them into bed?"

"Not at all. They melted in my arms as I kissed them on the lips and lightly caressed their breasts."

"And in bed...? Did they know anything?"

"A little guidance and they were perfect."

"And orgasm?"

"They experienced a powerful orgasm. I think they never experienced anything like it with any man."

My friend found the attitude of these girls, described as heterosexuals, to be perfectly normal. But I felt worried. These girls are repressing their own sexuality for years and years! Waiting for just a little touch! A fire waiting for two drops of water!

It is not true that girls become lesbians because men fail to make them contented. Girls become lesbians out of love for girls. How many men know how to caress with love! What men know extremely well is how to rape. If the mantra of patriarchy had not been artificially injected into their brains, if uncivilized cults and prayers had not blinded them, then most girls would have been lesbians. I too have experienced lesbianism and I can swear that in those days I was perfectly happy and contented, free from all worries and satisfied both within and without.

As soon as I returned to men, I was overcome with worry, distress, disquiet and dissatisfaction. Unfortunately, my body desires men; else I would have been a lesbian and could have shown the world how to love, how to live together, how to shout out in front of a million people: "I have every right to be a lesbian, I am a lesbian. I am not ashamed of myself, I am proud."

I feel sorry for those who live their whole life succumbing to the sexual desire of others. It is sad but true that these people form the majority in society.

The lesbian girl in Kolkata, who had come to tell me about her sufferings, had said that she was waiting for the grand day when, if ever, society would recognize lesbians. I told her that society would never do such a thing. I told her, "Don't give a damn. Speak up for your rights. Speak out loud. Homosexuals the world over, have fought for their rights; no one handed them their rights on a silver platter and said: 'here are your rights.' No society has ever been so humane."

Homosexuals must come out of their holes. As long as they remain burrowed in their holes, it will be easier for people to hate them, to fear them. Only if they come out, will people realize that they too are human beings, that they are their brothers and sisters, their near and dear ones.

The word 'lesbian' has been derived from 'Lesbo', an island in Greece in which 350 years before the birth of Christ a poet called Sappho was born. This poet was a woman and she expressed her love and sexual attraction for other women. In Bengali, we refer to lesbians as *samakami* or 'homosexuals'. It is a beautiful word, but it refers only to sex, it does not signify love. However, homosexual couples do love each other. Sex does not keep their relationship alive, love does. I have often seen homosexuals setting a far greater premium on love than heterosexuals.

American writer Rita May Brown, ex-girlfriend of tennis star Martina Navratilova, has said about lesbians that "girls who love girls are lesbians". Men, since they view women as sexual commodities, define lesbianism differently. According to them, lesbianism is the sexual relationship between two women. Brown has also said, "No government has the right to tell its citizens when or whom to love. The only queer people are those who don't love anybody."

Just as the government should not have the right to interfere in the love lives of the people, in the same breath it is the duty of the people to fight for their rights. Why are not those of us, who believe in human rights, not fighting for the enactment of civilized laws based on human rights for both homosexuals and non-homosexuals! How long shall we continue to believe in hatred, violence, war and bloodshed, and not believe in love! How long shall we scornfully condemn love, censor kisses and ban sexuality! How long shall we practise barbarism in the name of civilization?

***

27

Language my Mother

My mother taught me a language, her own language. In course of learning this language, I grew up and became an adult. Thanks to this language I spoke, I expressed my hunger and thirst, my longings and my aspirations. The language gave me the guts to say, 'I want my share.' In this language, I sang, I recorded my protest on the wall and unfolded my heart in my personal diary. Ultimately, nothing remained personal. Like a wild fire, it spread all over the country. The language gradually made me amazingly powerful. The language transformed me. I was no more a withdrawn, timid lass who spent time alone by counting the stars or wandering aimlessly. I started walking among the masses, breaking the man-made walls and uprooting the poison trees from the soil. I was strongly speaking not only for my own right but for the due share of millions of others.

This made them seethe in rage, and they tried to choke my voice and suppress my language.

They took away the pen from my hand and wished to make me dumb. They observed the festival of burning my books in towns and villages. They would make me dumb and speechless! They burnt me, but I ended up becoming steel instead of charcoal. They would seize the strength given by my Ma! Can anyone do that? Can the ruthless hands tear the sincere faith of a person? Can it destroy love? The language that flows in the blood? Is it possible to drain it out of the blood?

I was given banishment. I am abandoned, without a single friend or a dear one, but with me stays my tongue. In the macabre shadow of banishment, in exotic lands, in the crowd of alien people speaking different languages, I share my heart with my tongue in quietude. We spend sleepless nights and talk. I do not let my language get hurt by the hard clenched fists of alien languages. I do not let it get trampled down under the hairy feet of outlandish tongues. I keep the innocent solitary language under close guard, under constant watch. I safeguard her with love, and with my tears I clean the dust that settles on her. I am like her mother, her brother, her sister. She has been banished for more than a decade. She has been in ice, snow, in the darkness. Not in my tongue or ears, she has been in my heart all through these years. Isolated, kept away from the din and bustle, she was left in a corner just like me.

The language gradually falls prey to biting cold, freezes by the lashing whip of ice cold wind. I warm her by the heat of my bosom. I nurse her in the enemy camp. She is my dearest possession, she is my mother. Years passed by, many known faces bade me farewell, many dear ones crossed the boundary and went out of my sight. They would never return from that intractable distance. I am left alone; forlorn and exhausted. I have lost everything except the language. Thanks to the language I soliloquize with the people who deserted me. Because of her, I can write amidst this state of melancholy and loneliness. In pensive moments, I hide my face into the bosom of my language and shed tears. The language is there, so someone is there with me.

But the language longs for a locality, a country, warmth, the joy of pronunciation. I have come to this land (West Bengal), crossing huge distance, to save my language!

The language today sees the face of the sun; today she's a sunflower.

The language is today playing on the meadow under the afternoon sun, she's happy.

Now from her body the cluster of damp moss is eroding.

She's swimming in the Ganges, in the Bay of Bengal.

Removing the veil of tiring dependence in the alien territories, I and my dear language have now reached here, on the western side of my native land, and started living peacefully. We are home, in the safe repose. When I pronounce my language, I pronounce my mother. When I love my language, it seems like loving my mother. My mother is no more. I'm told by many that she has become a star in the sky.

In my mother's absence, my language looks after me so carefully. She is the language in which my mother spoke to me, loved me, wept for me, summoned me to her bosom. I closely hug my language and say, "You're my mom." In her I smell my mother's odour. My mother had no property or riches; the meagre possession she had crumbled and decayed. What remains to this day is her language, living and vivacious as ever.

I pronounce my mother, I'm pronouncing her. My language, I'll keep on pronouncing you as long as I shall breathe. I shall love you, as long as I am alive. I shall come back to you, wherever I go. I have always been without a shelter, so my tongue, take care of me. When after receiving blows and hatred I shall stoop down, my tongue, give me shelter, just like my mother used to give me.

I am writing in protestation. I am removing the hurdles from the path. Let the path be the path. The due share of women has been devoured by the villainous men. We women are now dumb, speechless. The more we want to speak, the more they gag our mouth and pour poison into our throat. They sew our lips and cut our tongues. For a thousand years, we have been speechless, sleepless; our backs bearing the signs of beatings. Let women be blessed with power of speech, let she be a spark, let her spread like fire. Let women burn and burn until they become as hard and powerful as steel.

Language, you're mother,

Language, you're me,

Language, you're sister.

Today women are pronouncing language, women are voicing protest. Women are using sharp, vitriolic language to register their protest and express their love for other women.

Today my language and I are moving freely. I warn nobody should try to come to shackle us, to stifle our independent voice, to pierce a knife into our loving hearts.

Power, stay off,

Power, don't throw stones,

Power, don't block the roads,

Power, learn to love,

Power, be human, if you can,

Power, be human and humane.

Allow me to live on my own sweet will, without any dispute, with love for my language. Allow me to live near my mother whose tears shall wash my dusty body. My mother's bosom is for me. In joy and sorrow I shall return into the warmth of her lap where she always had called me to come.

***

28

Wanted: Girls like Sanera

How many girls can do what Sanera, a girl from the village of Alunda in Birbhum, did? How many girls can take off their marriage garland bang in the middle of the marriage ceremony? An 18-year-old girl did indeed show her mettle. She refused to budge before anybody's request. She did what she wanted to do. She made the decision to break off her marriage and did just that. Sanera understood fully well that the man who did not hesitate to insult her father at the marriage ceremony would humiliate her at every step throughout her life. Sanera did not want that intolerable life, and that is why she chose to put paid to married life even before it began.

Sanera is only 18. At this age, girls are generally compelled to bow down before family pressure. It takes girls a long time to develop their language of protest. However, those who cannot develop it, cannot develop it ever in life. There are some who protest abundantly when they are teenagers, going about as they wish, keenly sensitive to their rights, but as soon as it is time for the thing called marriage, they shut their eyes, plug their ears and hang on to the groom chosen by their parents. Once at the in-laws', they are perfectly obedient daughters-in-law. Calm! Quiescent! Their naughty, daring, unruly teenage becomes a delectable memory, something like crispy snacks with afternoon tea.

According to the United Nations, two-thirds of all married women in India are victims of domestic violence. A new law against domestic violence has been enacted. But how many girls will take recourse to that law? Will girls other than the likes of Sanera dare to use the law against their persecuting husbands and drag them to prison? They will not dare, out of fear and shame. Fear and shame are as sacred to girls as their chastity. A girl who is not scared of society, one whom society cannot shame, is akin to one who has lost her modesty and chastity. Girls like Sanera are needed to make use of the law on domestic violence. Do such girls exist?

Sanera protested against an injustice. She did not care for the consequences. She did not get married. She does not care. Rather she said, "Is there any hard and fast rule that I must marry?" These are words, which, in this misogynistic society, ought to be a common refrain among girls. But even urban, educated and self-reliant girls do not utter such rich words as spoken by Sanera, daughter of a poor rickshaw puller in the village of Alunda. Sanera believes that she can live happily even without getting married. She says, "I know how to stitch, I'll embroider patterns on clothes. I'll work for a living the rest of my life." If girls had such self-confidence, the world would have been a different place. If a woman is determined that she will no longer spend her life with a persecuting husband, as Sanera did, and if she understands that she will be better off alone, without a husband than with a rogue, and if she finds a job for herself according to her skill, if she resolves to go ahead with self-respect intact, then truly the world is bound to change. But are there many girls like Sanera?

There are some marriages which involve the superstition of *lagna* auspicious moment of marriage). If the auspicious moment is missed by a fraction of a second, it spells disaster. Disaster not for the man, but for the woman. It is assumed that the person to whom a woman gets married will be her companion for life. No matter if all her life she simmers on the terrible fire of domesticity, or rots in the litter cast by man, she must not desert her partner. I have seen so many women in the Indian subcontinent, their faces distorted with grief and suffering, who can neither bear the pain nor do anything about it. And thus, valuable moments, valuable months of their lives pass. Long years go by, ages! Doesn't everyone privately dream of being a Sanera! Even if they do, most women do not have either the courage or the strength to realize that dream. Their dreams remain just that, dreams. Fear and shame guarantee that their dreams remain forever dreams.

It is a common belief that educated and self-reliant girls do not fall prey to domestic violence. Everyday girls are being tortured within the home, thus giving the lie to this belief.

These girls are doctors, engineers, lawyers, singers, actresses, entrepreneurs and what not! A girl who has graduated from school and college has to face the same kind of domestic violence that a girl who has not passed out from school or college. The reason is that both are women. Be they educated or uneducated, in the eyes of society, they are weak, they are the second sex. Sanera was ignorant of patriarchal theories. She simply knew what she wished to do. And she valued her wish. She shouted out. She broke off her marriage with a scoundrel. Sanera is surely not an educated girl, neither is she self-reliant. But she vehemently declared that she could become self-reliant. Parasitic girls, dependent on men, get cold feet when asked to fend for themselves. They include, in no mean numbers, girls who have graduated from college or university.

It is said that a man should kill a cat on the night of his marriage. Seeing the cat being beaten to death, the wife will remember that she too will be beaten in that manner. So she will be obsequious and humble, obey orders and instructions by the latter and dedicate her life to serving her husband. On the day of marriage, the groom's party beat up the bride's father rather than a cat and tried to convey the message: 'We give a fig for the father; imagine what we'll do to you!' Here Sanera's father does not represent men, he represents his daughter. That is why he tolerated the beating with such ease. If Sanera's father had been marrying off his son that day, nobody would have dared to hit him!

Sometimes such events that do not take place in a big city, occur in a small village, in the privacy of a small family. I have seen that it is in such small villages that a girl suddenly cuts off her rapist's penis, or elopes with a lover belonging to a different caste or a different religious community.

Uneducated girls like Sanera cannot imbibe the tenets of patriarchy like the girls who absorb it just as they learn history, geography, physics and chemistry. And so, girls like Sanera can easily say at their own marriage ceremony, 'I do not accept this marriage'. They are not at all embarrassed to stand firm and take off the marriage garland. They would have been embarrassed if they had imbibed the rules and regulations of patriarchy. Girls who have internalized the norms of patriarchy would not dare to break off a marriage even if the groom and his party had done something more terrible on the day of marriage, if they had not just beaten up the bride's father but killed him altogether. After all, disgrace is a terrible thing.

But Sanera does not know what constitutes disgrace. And so she did not hesitate to make such a difficult and important decision. What will happen to Sanera now? Her father will again try to get a match for her. Sanera will probably agree without a murmur. She will agree because her relatives and neighbours are simply not letting her be. Sanera will now dutifully serve her husband and in-laws and get thrashed every day. Either this will be the course of events, or Sanera will do as she said - refuse to marry and do something to earn a living. She is not fed or clothed by anybody. Neither does she care for any rules and customs. These are the two consequences I have thought of. Though I support the second, it is very difficult to accomplish that in this society. Will it be possible for Sanera to withstand, all by herself, the pressure to abide by the dictates of society, the censure she will face for having gone by her wish? If people everywhere had supported her, co-operated with her, then she would have got such moral courage. But I believe hundreds of girls today support Sanera, maybe not openly, but definitely deep in their hearts.

I congratulate Sanera. I do not know whether my congratulations will ever reach her. May be she will never know how much she has inspired me by her little act of resistance. I, who knows feminism inside out, have yet to learn a lot from Sanera. Men humiliate me in the most unpleasant manner possible, but I keep my mouth shut like a good, well-mannered girl, and because I keep my mouth shut, men do not find it the least bit difficult to insult and humiliate me again and again. I have this to learn that after being insulted once by men, I should not give them the chance to do it again, that I should the shut the door in their face.

***

29

364 Days for Men, One for Women

Woman's Day: How the day became ours:

8 March 1857: In New York, hundreds of woman workers employed in garment and textile industries gathered to protest their inhuman working conditions. They were forced to work for 12 hours for meagre wages. Police dispersed the procession of the protesting workers. Two years after the incident, those very workers formed a union.

8 March 1908: 15,000 women marched in procession in New York. Their demands included fewer working hours, better wages, right to vote and abolition of child labour. In May that year, the Socialist Party of America declared the last Friday of the month of February as National Women's Day.

28 February 1909: The first National Women's Day was celebrated in the whole of America. Women of America continued to celebrate this day till 1913.

1910: Women in Europe began to celebrate the last Sunday of the month of February as Women's Day.

In Copenhagen, the capital of Denmark, the demand for an international women's day was raised at the conference of the Socialist International Women. Clara Zetkin, leader of the German Socialist Party, played a leading role in it. One hundred women representatives from 17 countries supported the proposal of an international women's day. Till then, no definite date for an international women's day was fixed.

19 March 1911: International Women's Day was celebrated in Europe with great pomp and grandeur. In Austria, Germany, Switzerland and Denmark, over 10 lakh women marched in procession with the demand for their rights - the right to vote, the right to participate in politics, the right to work. They demanded abolition of the discrimination prevalent between men and women at the workplace.

Only a few days after this, 140 women workers were burned to death in an accident in New York. Most of the women were Italians and Jews. This incident triggered off a tumultuous workers' movement in America.

8 March 1913-1914: In Europe and America, International Women's Day began to be celebrated on this date. Women began to protest against the First World War.

23 February 1917: 20 lakh Russian women marched in procession with the demand for bread and peace and in protest against grinding poverty. At that time, Russia used to follow the Julian calendar. 23 February in the Julian calendar was 8 March in the Georgian calendar.

8 March 1975: The United Nations declared this day as the International Women's Day.

December 1977: The General Assembly of the United Nations seconded a proposal that all member states would have to accept a day as United Nations Day for Women's Rights and International Peace Day.

The Day Now

The day is not as political today as it used to be. It is now a day like any odd Father's Day, Mother's Day or Valentine's Day.

What happens across the country on this day? Lengthy speeches are delivered at various meetings in different countries. Glitzy rallies are held in different countries. Happy and contented women dress up to the tees. They eat, drink and have a jolly time.

A lot else also happens on this day, about which few people get to know anything at all. Numerous girls go hungry for want of food; they go thirsty for want of potable water. They even die.

On this day, female foetuses are killed so as to ensure that daughters are not born. On this day, unwanted daughters are born, causing great sorrow to their families. On this day, hundreds of women are given *talaq* by their husbands for committing the crime of giving birth to baby girls.

On this day, infant girls are murdered because they are girls. Infant girls are abandoned in garbage heaps because they are girls. On this day, elderly men rape infant girls.

On this day, teenage girls, young girls, are gangraped in villages, marts, cities and ports. On this day, men douse girls in kerosene and set fire to them. On this day, men strangle girls to death. On this day, men savagely beat up girls. Men throw acid on the face of girls. Boyfriends sell their girlfriends in red light areas. On this day, millions and millions of girls are trafficked from one country to another, from one city to another, from one village to another, to be used as sex slaves or simply slaves. On this day, countless girls who have been trampled, stung, slighted, neglected and dishonoured commit suicide in attempt to safeguard their dignity.

On this day, those people whose demand (supply is organized only when there is demand, if there is no demand there is no need of supply) has caused crore of girls to become prostitutes or sex slaves, feast on our miserable, victims-of-patriarchal-politics girls to their heart's content. Girls are crushed under male violence from the dawn of Women's Day till midnight, a violence which is a thousand times more ruthless than inhuman and bestial violence.

364 Men's Days, 1 Women's Day:

Actually, to tell the truth, in this male-dominated society all 365 days are Men's Days. One day has been set aside for women out of charity. Since women are atrociously tormented by men, a day is reserved for women to gather in hordes and cry buckets. Or, they can gather together and organize seminars along the lines of 'Lord and Master, we are perfectly happy with what you have given us'. The age of 'Down with…,' 'We do not accept…' slogans is long gone. Now it is considered good grace to be soft and compromising. The art and strategy of making women gracious is nothing new in this society.

In this world, there is no necessity of having a separate day earmarked as Men's Day. Because, every day is a Man's Day.

My own opinion is that if the horrible discrimination prevalent between man and woman is abolished, then there will be no day called Women's Day or Men's Day. My dream is to have all 365 days as Human Days.

No, not many people have criticized this day. Not even feminists of repute have criticized it. American politician, feminist and lawyer Bella Abzug, known for speaking her mind, has said something quite wonderful:

> "They used to give us a day – it was called International Women's Day. In 1975 they gave us a year, the Year of the Woman. Then from 1975 to 1985 they gave us a decade, the Decade of the Woman. I said at the time, who knows, if we behave they may let us into the whole thing. Well, we didn't behave and here we are." Whenever there is talk of 'behaving' I am reminded of the famous quote: 'Well-behaved women rarely make history."

What shall we Women do Now

We have been given a day. We shall celebrate that day. Some of us will say: We are all perfectly fine, but in back-of-beyond villages, maybe a few girls are not all that fine; actually they do not get their rights because they do not make an effort. What can you not do if you really wish to do it!

Some of us will say we are not fine. We are being oppressed inside and outside the home. Patriarchy and religion, prejudice and domestic life, custom and purdah, tradition and culture – in this society all these are anti-women. Woman is nothing but a sexual commodity in this society; woman is meant to serve man and his cult and prayer. A revolution is needed to smash this religious, patriarchal, rotten, old, prejudiced society and create a new society in which there will be no discrimination.

Some will say, if there is to be a revolution, only women must come forward.

Some will say, both men and women have to come forward.

Some will sing paeans to prostitution. Some will want to wipe out prostitution. Women themselves will speak in favour of commodification of women; again, many women will speak against commodification of women. The two sides will express two different views. And no unity will be forged among women. Women will be divided. Women will be split into two. This year, too, as in all other years. What better way to keep patriarchy alive and kicking for a thousand years more!

***

30

Little Details of Everyday Life

I

There was a show called 'Bodyline' on television. A man was shooting questions while two star-women fielded those. The man was asking them about male cricketers—who do they find sexy, who they wish to marry, who they find most appealing. The girls were merrily answering these questions. When asked what kind of man they would like in private life, both replied that they would like aggressive men. They are just not satisfied if men are not aggressive.

I just gaped at the TV set. No, not men, but women who were seeking aggressive men. Aggressiveness in men is everywhere in this male-dominated society. Men are raping women, gang-raping them, killing female foetuses, kidnapping and murdering women; the incidence of wife-killing is on the rise; two-thirds of all married women admit to being victims of domestic violence; men are throwing acid at women, cheating on them, leading them out of their houses in the guise of lovers and selling them into prostitution; trafficking in women is rising day by day; men are dousing women in kerosene and setting them on fire, they are beheading women and floating their heads in rivers, murdering them and then hanging the body from the ceiling fan to pass it for suicide. Thanks to the aggressiveness of men, violence against women is rampant in the villages and in the towns and the cities, at home and outside. And the sexy sirens are talking about their desire for aggressive men! They want macho men. Rough and tough. They want powerful muscles, they want muscular strength—that muscular strength with which men can overwhelm the weak, that is women. Man's job is to keep woman in his fist, dominate over her, knock her out cold with a snap of the fingers if she tries to be smart. Women love to be crushed in the muscles of men, and in this way greatly help in keeping patriarchy alive. It is these women who inspire countless women to desire men, aggressive men. They are bowled over by aggressiveness in men. So when a man gives a violent kick to her desire, when he clutches her by the hair and tears it off, when he smashes her forehead, when he gives her a bloody eye, the girl is quite giddy with joy. If a man doesn't behave like this, he is a wimp!

Women love to be masochists, they adore being tortured. For how many ages, how many centuries will silly, stupid women continue to sacrifice themselves to fulfil the wishes of men, to satisfy their whims and give them more and more pleasure!

‖

The girl who used to help me with my household work had gone home on a long leave. I was alone at home. I was doing my household chores by myself. In the meanwhile, a few female friends came over to my place. After dinner, they washed up the utensils they had used. Not only so, they voluntarily helped me with some other housework and even left behind food they had brought from home. They guessed that I had problems managing all the housework on my own and helped me in every way they could, like real friends do. A couple of days later, a few male friends, who were quite as close as my female friends, came to my house. They hung around the place, drank, ate and scattered things about, creating mayhem all around. When I asked them to tidy up the place, they started in surprise. I told them very politely that the girl who helped me with the housework was not there and as I remain busy, I would not have the time to clear up the clutter. They were not the least bit sympathetic. Rather, they laughed aloud, as if I had said something really funny. I explained to them I was not joking, I really wanted them to put everything back in its proper place. I took my friends to the kitchen and tried to get them to do the wash-up. I couldn't. They thought I insulted them. They wetted the commode seat by peeing without lifting the seat and came off without flushing. When I protested, they laughed nastily. I do not understand how they can have a domestic life with this sort of manners. I shudder to think of the wretched condition of their wives.

These men, however, are known as respectable men in society. They think that cleaning up the house and keeping it tidy is women's work. And their work lies in having a good time, making merry, sitting tight, lying in bed and issuing orders: I want this, I want that.

Women are relegated to the status of untouchables because of certain advantages patriarchy gives to men. It is the task of a man's grandmother, aunt, mother, sister, sister-in-law, wife, lover, girlfriend, servant and scavenger to clean up the scraps or leftovers of his meal.

Unless there is a change in this attitude of men, there will be no change in our society. The relationship between man and woman will continue to remain a master-servant relationship. If there is discrimination in human society, it is the responsibility of both men and women to eliminate it, not of anyone alone. If there is to be equality and healthiness in human society, both man and woman have to take part in this mission. Otherwise, the mental illness of men, the disease that makes them think of themselves as kings and emperors and belonging to a superior class than women, will never be cured.

III

I saw Deepa Mehta's *Water*. An extraordinary movie. How beautifully she has portrayed the dominance of religion, the sufferings of girls, the agony of widowhood! How heart-rending those scenes are where an eight-year-old girl is draped in widow's white and shoved into a home for widows! How heart-rending is the scene in which the girl has been raped and abandoned in a boat! The boat drifts along. Just as the world drifts along unperturbed and undisturbed!

For 500 years, elderly widows, and even child-widows, are being abandoned, as if in the hope that they die soon.

The movie, *Water*, is based on events that took place about 70 years ago. The pathetic story of widows in ashrams in Kashi has been depicted in it. Maybe the torture that was inflicted on girls at that time is not there in that degree today, but is it totally absent? Girls here—educated, trendy Kolkata girls—know that Indian girls are extremely independent. Nobody in the world has enjoyed the kind of independence that Hindu girls enjoy. There is a law in favour of widow remarriage, so there is nothing to worry about. But have they ever peeped into Kashi-Vrindavan to see how hundreds of widows are suffering over there! Have they ever looked at the bland boiled fare (*habishyi*) widows in every odd home in Kolkata are compelled to partake?

No! Anti-women superstitions will never be wiped out of society. Patriarchy will triumph in a society where there is no culture of equality between men and women.

IV

I have seen a couple or so episodes of a few serialized plays on television. It is surprising that the girls in these plays wear loud make up even when they are shown at home, doing housework, or when they get up from sleep or when they go to bed. They are also dressed to the tees. I told a few directors of television serials that it just did not match with the reality. Do women dress up so much when they are simply sitting at home? The director replied, "I have no alternative. If women do not dress up in that manner the TRP slides down, viewers don't like to see drab and pale-faced girls."

But does that mean, they will have to go to sleep with lipstick, rouge, eye-shadow and eyeliner on, a big bindi on the forehead and tonnes of ornaments to boot?

The directors said, yes.

Surely, this rule does not apply to men? They shook their heads, no.

Why can't they make do with the way girls really are? Why must girls need extra colours, extra mannerisms? Why do girls have to shed fat from different parts of their body and get the figure prescribed by fashion magazines, fashion shows or the world of advertisements? Has anybody ever asked these questions? Minus physical beauty and again beauty as defined by men women are thought to be rather unattractive and worthless. That is why women are being compelled to adopt a host of measures to stay beautiful. In this patriarchal society, men can display their personality, their qualities, their knowledge of complex things, their skill, expertise and so on. On the other hand, women have nothing to exhibit but their bodies. Everything in woman is insignificant compared to her body. The things that are supposed to be qualities in a woman are considered so because that's what men need and that's how they can keep woman in subjugation. For instance, cooking, housework; for instance, sewing, serving, sympathy, extreme dependence; for instance, meek and humble ways; for instance, shame and fear.

Women have no lives of their own. If a woman holds a big post in a big company, if she is a director, if she is a proprietor, if she is immensely successful in business, if a woman is a top doctor, engineer, scientist, or astronaut, or a leading writer, or artist, or a hotshot politician, economist or sociologist, only then is she able to earn the respect of all members of society. The success, which a woman earns without exhibiting her body or using it is true success. But success is never considered as a quality in women. The posts are masculine. Top posts or the top strata are never feminine, which is why people have endless respect for these posts, respect for these masculine posts. Whoever sits in this post is held in esteem; if it is a woman, then she too is held in esteem. But this is not respect for a woman as a human being. This is respect for the height she has scaled, respect for success—the synonym of which height or success is masculinity.

***

31

Women = Body

The thought that crossed my mind after watching *Nishabd* was whether the opposite could have happened. An 18-year-old boy in love with a 60-year-old woman: could this be the storyline for a movie? No, it could not. No matter how old a man is, how hideously ugly, he is still a man. He is noble, he is great. It is easy to fall in love with greatness. A 60-year-old woman—no matter what she is, erudite, talented, having an attractive personality, whatever—she has only one identity: she is an old woman, an old woman with wrinkled skin. A woman is judged by her body. If the body goes to the dogs, so does the lady. Not so for a man. Amitabh, with all his wrinkles, can well play the lover of a teenager, can majestically rule the whole country as a megastar. But Madhabi, with her wrinkles, can be anything but a star. Despite his wrinkled skin, Soumitra Chattopadhyay romps about the town every bit a star. But Suchitra Sen has to remain in self-imposed exile year after year. Rekha has to do away with her wrinkles in order to carry on, but Amitabh doesn't need to do that.

These are just examples. The problem lies not with the world of cinema, but with society. That a girl's asset is her beauty is a completely political idea or belief. It is political because it perpetuates the patriarchal system. If a girl's beauty is not considered to be her asset, then her education, awareness, knowledge, intellect, skill, judgment, and other such qualities would become not of secondary, but primary importance. And that would be dangerous for patriarchy. It would no longer be possible to control a woman by treating her as a doll.

If any system has to be kept alive in society for a long, long time, then it must be backed by shrewd politics. Raising a child in an environment of gender-based discrimination right from birth, and drilling in him/her the teaching—like man is superior, woman backward, man is intelligent, woman stupid, man is the master, woman the servant—is a political and not a social process. The politics of patriarchy is so strong and tough that though cracks develop in capitalism, though socialism collapses, patriarchy stands as it always did, stronger than ever before.

Nothing belonging to a woman is her own. Even her own life is not her own. Woman is the property of man, not just of man but of this male-dominated society. Society keeps a close watch over her to check if her hymen is intact, whether or not her dress and conduct pass muster, whether or not she is married off within marriageable age, whether or not she waits on her husband hand and foot as she should, whether or not she has given birth to sons, and whether or not she is living life as a

chaste and loving wife who brings prosperity to her husband
and his family. If she cannot satisfy society, society arranges for
her punishment. Quite a harsh punishment.

The spotlight that used to be on the chastity of women has
now shifted, particularly in the Western countries, on a woman's
figure. In Eastern countries, while the chastity of women
continues to be under surveillance, now a girl's body is also
under close scrutiny. Rules are laid down as to what the neck,
shoulders, chest, stomach, lower abdomen, hips and legs should
be like in form. If a girl does not live up to the specifications,
she is threatened and censured, pitied and disgraced. Young
girls suffer from bulimia and anorexia because they go on diet
in order to ensure they are not shelved in the girl-mart. Girls
labour tirelessly to get this curve or that crease in different zones
of their bodies just right. The crease must be at exactly the right
spot, and if it occurs elsewhere, then it has to be straightened
out with an expensive anti-creasing ointment; and if that does
not work, one has to rush for cosmetic surgery.

Think of all the famous 19th Century water colours and
sculptures based on female models. When we see them today,
does not it appear as if all the girls were nine months' pregnant!
The female figure, which was thought as normal only some time
back, is now considered abnormal. Women have never been able
to decide what kind of figure they should have. Those modern
women who have earned fame as collaborators of patriarchy
have now taken up the responsibility of dressing up the other
girls. The responsibility of presenting commodities before men,
in an even more attractive package.

Women are beautiful—this is a strong political weapon used against women's progress. There is tremendous pressure on women to remain beautiful and never be classified as ugly. So they have to work day and night like donkeys, and spend enormously on cosmetics. How many crores of rupees worth cosmetics are women compelled to use everyday! A flourishing market is out there for so many colours for the face, cheeks, nose, eyes, eyebrows, hair, chin, so many chemicals, so many kinds of paste, so many kinds of dye. Why? Isn't the face one has enough? Are the cheeks, eyes and eyebrows not perfect? Are girls born imperfect? Are they born abnormal? Are they born deformed? Is that why they have to shed this and enhance that, wear this and discard that in order to become perfect, in order to heal their deformity! These girls who shoulder the burden of making themselves perfect surely feel that without all these they are just not perfect or complete. They accept this lie either consciously or unconsciously. Accepting this lie means denying women their due as human beings. Accepting this lie means hating girls, insulting them abominably and actively participating in the politics of commoditization of girls.

There are advertisements all over the place telling us how girls should look. Not just advertisements, but also the cinema, television, billboards, journals and dolls. There is no escaping it. Girls have been so trapped in the snare of beauty that they have to spend their entire lives taking care of their looks, they have to spend everything they earn on it. They will have no time to think of their rights and their deprivations. They will become penniless in their attempts to groom themselves, all their savings will go down the drain. Our kids have got caught in a wicked trap. A sample survey will reveal that 90 per cent of girls think they are not beautiful enough, their breasts are too small, legs too skinny, waist fat, buttocks out of shape, hair too wispy, complexion dark, nose blunt, eyes small and skin wrinkled. Girls are becoming increasingly disappointed and upset over one or other part of their body. The politics of making girls lose their confidence is dangerous. If girls lack in confidence, if they are continuously afraid and worried about their selves, the courage and strength to challenge patriarchy vanishes into thin air. The consciousness that is very important for the sake of their liberty too dies and rots away.

The saddest thing is that if education and self-reliance take girls a step forward, it also pushes them two steps backward. These girls are getting increasingly disappointed with their bodies and this disappointment is prodding them to expend all their talent on their bodies. Bidding goodbye to originality, they try to drape their bodies in all that is artificial so that the figure coincides exactly with the figure suggested by the alliance of patriarchy, the media and the cosmetics trade. If her figure matches the ideal perfectly, then it is a victory for the girl. That is how women have learnt to abandon their intelligence and common sense.

Not just the grandmothers of today's girls, their mothers and grandmothers too were far more free. They did not have to face the pressure of being beautiful. It was enough for them to have the quality required to be a maidservant. But now it is not enough to be a maidservant, one must be a beautiful servant too. You cannot pass if your bust, waist and legs are not of the correct size. If your skin is not supple, if it is not of just the right complexion, you will not pass. The world belongs to men, society belongs to men, and here a woman is nothing but a body.

It is the law of patriarchy to crumple and crush the rights of women due to them as human beings; to deny the distinct and individual existence of women; to make use of women in its own interest; to attach no value to women. Whenever the women's rights movement attempts to enhance the worth of women, the sacred duty of patriarchy is to see to it that their worth is immediately undermined.

When the value of women starts to decline, a woman's body becomes her only identity card, by displaying which she can get through the life. When their value goes down, women tend to dress up carefully, the number of beauty parlours shoots up. When their value goes down, there is a hike in the money demanded as dowry. Housewife-ness increases. Prostitution increases. Female foeticide increases. Domestic violence increases. Rape increases. Murder of women increases. It is because the value of women in society is so minimal that all kinds of anti-women deeds are done unhindered and in peace.

When women become nothing but a body consisting of shape and beauty, their life turns into something extremely trivial. The voice that shouts for equal rights also chokes on its own. Is it possible to shout abuses after having swallowed the bait? Is it possible to flare up in protest after having compromised?

Possibly, patriarchy has not been so successful in any conspiracy as it has been in setting women against women.

***

32

Female Foeticide: Only Men will Stay Alive in India

Generally the ratio between women and men is such that there are more women than men—something like 1,005 women for every 1,000 men. This is the picture in any healthy society. But if society is diseased, the ratio is likewise skewed. A few communities in India were already suffering from this disease, but now it has acquired the proportions of an epidemic. Believe it or not, this is the truth.

Back in 1992, when Jayalalitha was the chief minister of Tamil Nadu, she initiated a 'swing' system. According to this scheme, people could leave their unwanted daughters on the swing. That year, 77 infants made their way to the swing, of which only 20 survived to be adopted. Nobody could pin their faith on this system. It was found that between April and December 1993, 1,194 girls were born in that particular region of Tamil Nadu, 156 infant girls were killed, 243 infanticides were prevented and only 7 infants were brought to the swing. The swing project was finally scrapped.

Girls have always enjoyed more respect in South India than in the northern part of the country. In fact, once upon a time in Kerala, a matriarchal society existed. The daughter would inherit the property of the mother. After marriage, a girl would not go to her husband's home. She would stay put in her own house, enjoying immense power, and the husband would sometimes come and spend a few days with her. Even after that matriarchal society collapsed, girls in Kerala continued to enjoy more regard and respect than in any other state in the country. There were more girls than boys. The girls were more educated, more self-reliant. However, it is in that girls' paradise, Kerala, that infant girls are now being murdered. Tamil Nadu, Andhra Pradesh and Karnataka are also changing, particularly Tamil Nadu. In some villages of this state, girls are being murdered in a planned way, if possible, before they are born; if not, then after. Usilampatti, Salem, Dharampur, North Arcot, Periyar, Dindigul and Madurai are identified as zones of female infanticide. In some regions of Tamil Nadu, there is supposed to be a tradition of female infanticide. The drop of milk that mother and grandmother put in the mouth of a newborn girl is mixed with the dust of yellow oleander. Those who are rather scientific-minded grind sleeping pills and add the powder to the milk, or use a little pesticide. Infant girls are killed not in these regions only, but throughout the country. However, the *modus operandi* varies from place to place. In Gujarat, mothers drown baby girls in milk. In Punjab, the girl is stuffed inside an earthen vessel, the lid is shut tight and the vessel buried underground. Many people do not know that it is a crime to kill infant girls. Many communities think it is the most natural thing in the world.

Infanticide is barbaric. Then again, nowadays, the police are creating a lot of trouble. So the safest thing is female foeticide. Since it does not look barbaric, there is no question of a guilty conscience. Scanning is quite cheap now. Modern methods of sex determination and abortion have penetrated interior villages too. Previously, people would run from temple to temple, pleading with god for a son. They would spend extravagantly on saints and hermits, but now there is no need of charms and spells since a medium even stronger than god has come to India: science. Scan machines, amniocentesis and other scientific tests reveal the sex of the embryo in the womb; if the sex is not right, then it is got rid of. The right sex is masculine, the wrong sex feminine. The healthy sex is masculine, the disabled sex feminine.

Women of Tamil Nadu admit to murdering their daughters, but they are not at all sorry. They feel no remorse. Mothers, angry and in tears, ask: "What do you want? What shall we do with our daughters? Why should we let them live? So that they are tortured like us? So that they suffer throughout their lives, like we are suffering?"

Girls in our society grow up learning that their lives are of no value; if they cannot give pleasure to and satisfy men, then they will be chastised by society as inefficient, worthless and good-for-nothing creatures. It is indeed true that knowledge, intellect, sensibility, skill and efficiency in women are not conferred any value; women are regarded as sexual commodities, weak of

Female Foeticide: Only Men Will Stay Alive in India   201

character and an inferior race. Knowing full well how intolerable life can be for a girl, women crave for sons; they do not want daughters. Pressure from the family as well as society compels women to kill their infant daughters or the female foetus. It is true that women participate in the killing rites, but why should we blame them! They are mere pawns in this game. Such murder is a crime in the eyes of the law. But instead of punishing the actual offender, women are being punished nowadays. In this society of hideous gender discrimination, if women are blamed for foeticide or infanticide, then they are actually being punished twice—first, for being born as a girl, and secondly, for thwarting the birth of a girl. Why do women commit murder? Because if they give birth to a girl, they are kicked for it, if they give birth to multiple daughters, they are thrown out of the house by the husband, and they have no place in their father's house either. So by murdering the daughter, they save not only the girl, but also themselves.

Though banned by law, foeticide and infanticide are going on in full swing. Violence against women is also banned by law. Isn't it going on? Whose law prevails within the four walls of the house? It is the law of the male master that holds sway there. Is there any girl who, in this male-dominated society, can lodge a complaint against a man and yet go scot-free? Who will let her live the rest of her life?

In 1992, a scheme was launched in Tamil Nadu for the safety of infant girls. It targeted eradication of infanticide by 2000. Couples with one or two daughters and no son would be given a monetary award if one of the parents opted for sterilization.

The money would be kept in fixed deposit account in the name of the daughter till she reached the age of 21. Schooling expenses of the daughter would be sent to her parents. Twenty thousand families were to be brought within the ambit of the scheme each year. In 1992, 641 girls from the district of Salem received the money for one-and-a-half years. Finally, the scheme had to be scrapped. There were too many hindrances and hazards. Roughnecks, policemen, usurers, and bribe takers wreaked havoc with the scheme. When the money deposited in the girl's name would be withdrawn—when she would turn 21— it would not be used for anything other than dowry. No scheme can perhaps bring about any real change in the condition of girls.

Till the age of six, the ratio between boys and girls ought to be at least 1000:950. As the age increases, this ratio also changes; the number of girls increases, while the number of boys decreases. This is because girls are capable to live longer than boys. If girls get care and attention, then the ratio becomes 1005:1000 in their favour. If girls get equal rights, then they greatly outnumber boys. But if the number of girls is less than 950 till the age of six, it is to be understood that they are definitely being killed.

A research conducted by Amartya Sen reveals 30,700,000 girls were missing in India in 1986. It is not as if these girls went missing all of a sudden. It is a long history of craving for sons. For many years, the number of girls in India has been less than in any other country. The 1901 census revealed that as far as adult women were concerned, there were 972 girls for every 1,000 boys. The number of girls has been decreasing since then. In 2001, the number of girls was 933, i.e., for every 1,000 boys, there were 70 girls less. So the figures boil down to this —in a country of 100 crores, 70,000,000 girls were murdered that year. In India there is no state where the number of girl child has not fallen. In some states, such as Punjab, Haryana, Himachal Pradesh, Gujarat, and Maharashtra, the number has dipped below 800 for 1,000 boys. In Gurudaspur in Punjab, there are 729 girls for 1000 boys. In Mehsana in Gujarat, the number is 752. In Salem, Tamil Nadu, the number is 763, and in Ambala, Haryana, it is 772. In Shahjahanpur, Uttar Pradesh, it is 678. In these areas, 200 girls out of every 1,000 go missing. In Punjab and Haryana, the alarm bells were supposed to have started ringing from 1991. However, no one perhaps imagined how far the figure could decline in 10 years. In 1991, no state had fewer than 800 girls per 1,000 boys, but in 10 years' time, four states already had less than 800 girls.

The NGOs say that if women are educated and can earn, then female infanticide and female foeticide will stop. Most people believe that planned infanticides occur among the poor and the uneducated. But, in fact, the opposite is true. In India the ratio of girls to boys is the most skewed in South Delhi, a place where the rich and the educated live. It is here that the maximum number of girls had gone missing—down from 904 to 845 in just 10 years. Twenty four thousand girl child disappear from South Delhi every year. The Patels of Gujarat are a wonder. Traditionally rich peasants, there is no trace of girls in their villages. In Chandigarh, the number of girls is 853. In Chandigarh city, the number is even less, 844. In India, the proportion of girls is lesser in rich and educated areas than in poor and uneducated regions. More girls are murdered in those areas. There is a holocaust going on against girls across the country, a pogrom. In West Bengal, more girls disappear in Kolkata than in any other regions.

There were 10,000,000 female foeticides in India in the last two decades. In 1997, the 50th anniversary of Indian Independence, 500,000 girls were denied the right to be born on this soil—in a country which boasts of being the world's largest democracy.

In this country, girls are fast becoming extinct. Anti-women superstitions have been carefully nurtured over the ages. There are quite a few communities, which regard only sons as offspring, and not daughters. Till 1980, infant girls used to be killed after they were born. Foeticide had not caught on. Despite being banned, the incidence of foeticide is on the rise. It makes one afraid that as long as the status of girls in society does not improve, there is no way these murders, this bloodshed, can be prevented. The condition in North India is so dreadful that it is feared there will be no girls by year 2021.

Securing girls from a host of problems such as harassment, torture and oppression through murder is nothing new. This tradition goes back many, many years. Girls have learnt for a long time now that their greatest security in this society lies in not remaining alive. It was the British who identified zones of female infanticide in their kingdom. The British found out that around 1805, female infanticide was prevalent among the Jadejas of Saurashtra. At that time, there was a village in Eastern Uttar Pradesh, in which not a single girl could be found. In 1808, the ruler of Baroda, Alexander Walker, sent summons to the chief of every community asking them to sign a bond that they would not commit female infanticide anymore. In 1870, measures were taken to prevent female infanticide. In 1898, the government declared female infanticide a crime. A law for the prevention of female infanticide had once been enacted, but was later repealed for political reasons.

Anthropologists say that from the beginning of civilization, whenever there has been scarcity of food, women and children have been killed. Darwin said that girls used to be killed at birth, not because it was necessary for them to die so that society may live, but because the male-dominated society regarded them as a burden.

There are documented records of villages in 19th century India that had no infant girls. Some regions had 343 boys against 54 girls. Bombay had 1838 boys and 603 girls. If we go back even further, what will we find? Killing of a girl child was probably in vogue during the Vedic age. The *Atharva Veda* says, 'Let girl children be born elsewhere, let boy children take birth here. Son is wealth. Son is a blessing. The son will be the father's strength in old age. The father will go to heaven if the son lights his funeral pyre. It is the son who will rescue the father from hell.'

What is the role of women? A woman is the soil on which a man will sow his seeds to produce a son. According to Manu, girls must depend on men day and night. He said, the father will protect her when she is a child, her husband when she is a young woman and her son when she is old. Freedom is not for women. Women do not deserve it.

First, girls are being asked to remain dependent on others. Then they are being told that they are a kind of burden. However, one thing that is true is that from the ancient times till today girls have been kept as the private property of men.

Since infant girls have been murdered over the ages, female foeticide today does not go against tradition. It is like weeding—plucking off girls from the soil of the womb reserved for the production of sons. There is nothing surprising about murdering daughters in a race that is thirsty for sons.

Ramchandra's father, King Dasharath, fed his three wives some pudding and immediately the wives gave birth to four sons. In some regions of Southern India, wives are even now fed that magic pudding of mythology, so that they give birth to sons.

According to some, Sita was a victim of the societal custom of female infanticide, but was later rescued. King Janak retrieved the infant Sita from an earthen vessel buried underground. It was the tradition of the place where Sita was found, to stuff a live infant girl inside a vessel, put in a string and a chunk of molasses, and then shut the lid tight, bury the vessel under the ground and cry out loud, eat the molasses, stay put there, never return, send your brother. Probably, both Ram and Sita are products of the ancient form of sex selection.

There is no difference in races and religions when it comes to craving for a son. Emperor Akbar sought the blessings of Salim Chisti for a son. A son was born. He was named Salim and a magnificent city called Fatehpur Sikri was built to celebrate his birth.

In every nook and cranny, lane and by-lane of this country, there are *dharmashalas*, where one can go and pray for a son.

206 *Taslima Nasreen No Country for Women*

Hindu, Sikh, Muslim or Buddhist—everybody needs a son. India is overflowing with godmen. People have had their fill of genuflecting before godmen, they have had their fill of fakirs and quacks. Neither god nor godman is perfect. Science is perfect. Science has now arrived to deliver people from magic spells and charms, from gods and godmen. Prayers to god and a variety of religious rites and rituals never yielded the fruit that science yields. Science has enabled people to identify the gender of the child in the womb. If the gender is not to one's liking, the foetus will be taken care of. Such an obnoxious union of tradition and technology cannot be seen anywhere else on the earth.

In the beginning scientists claimed that science can put paid to many an unwanted pregnancy. The method of scanning was already there, next came amniocentesis. This was chiefly meant to detect any abnormality or deformity in the foetus. But in India it is not used for that purpose. It is used to detect the gender of the foetus. As soon as it is evident that the gender is feminine, it is bidden goodbye. Thus, the attitude of this country is that the abnormality of the foetus lies in its gender, deformity lies in the gender itself, in the feminine gender.

There are two kinds of abortions, legal and illegal. A thin line separates the two. Abortion is legal, but abortion after sex determination is illegal. A girl can legally opt for an abortion if there is any abnormality in the foetus. But what is the difference between normal and abnormal? A healthy and normal female foetus is as good as—or as bad as—what, according to medicine and science, is an abnormal foetus. Socially, both foetuses are unwanted.

If an abnormal or deformed foetus, or a female foetus, is allowed to be born, it entails immense expenses. It entails mental instability for the parents, as also economic collapse. So it is better that they are not allowed to be born. Such is the opinion of those who believe that female foeticide is justified.

The abortion clinics display an advertisement—Spend Rs 500, save Rs 50,000. In other words, 'Kill this one. If this one lives, you'll lose Rs 50,000 in dowry.' In 2005 alone, ultrasound factories worth Rs 500 crore were built. For those yearning for a son, the sex determination clinics are modern temples.

Girls in Europe and America have had to struggle for long years for the right of abortion. Acquiring the right of abortion was a huge event in the history of women's emancipation. However, in India, when a foetus is aborted by virtue of belonging to a certain gender and that gender is the feminine gender, then such an abortion has nothing to with women's liberty. It is inseparably related with the tragedy of women's subjugation.

Whichever country Indians may go to live in, they invariably take with them a piece of India. They may live in Europe or America, but their craving for a son does not die. They come to India for abortion, because it is cheaper here than there. They have discovered other varieties of tests and investigations. They take recourse to modern methods of detecting disease in the foetus in order to find out, on the sly, the sex of the foetus. If the foetus is not of the correct gender, then invariably it will be murdered. The number of girl children in Indian families in New Jersey is no more than in Punjab and Haryana. Indian girls now run the risk of becoming extinct. They are an endangered species, more so than the tiger.

Some people have tried to talk law. Those girls who have killed their own children, cried out, 'Law, what is law? Will the law come to my aid when my husband throws me out of the house for giving birth to yet another girl! Will the law help me when my husband marries again in the hope of a son? Can the law change the way society looks at me because I have no son?'

Female infanticide of yore has now been replaced by modern sex selective abortion. DNA test, pre-genetic diagnosis test and so much more hi-tech. Society must be devoid of girls. It simply is a must. Society is not prepared to respect the girl child. But the law says that a girl child cannot be murdered. In the meanwhile, women go on explaining why they murder their own children. The reason is that society wants sons, the family wants sons. If a woman cannot provide a son, her life is being torn by strife. To put it bluntly, the message flashed by society—and this is what people really think, no matter what they say—is that, if you have two sons, you have two eyes. If you have one son, you are blind in one eye. And if you have two daughters, you are completely blind. The law is being violated. Everybody is breaking the law—Doctors, nurses, midwives, laboratories, hospitals. Though sex determination tests were officially banned in 1994, nobody seems to care. It becomes difficult to implement the law when the attitude of the people does not change. Again, the outlook too will not change as long as the law is not enacted. The question is, are people born with this attitude, this anti-women attitude? No, this attitude is acquired.

When crime is on the rise in society, the value of girls crashes drastically. Who knew that the scan machines would become instruments of murder! Female infanticide is making a comeback in Punjab and Haryana, because female foeticide is growing tougher day by day. Not only it is illegal, the NGOs too are lying in wait to nab the offender. Nurses and midwives are particularly evil in those villages where the number of infant girls is few. These ambassadors of birth are actually turning out to be the agents of death.

Why are girls opting for abortion, why are they not letting infant girls live? The girls say, 'Why should we let them live? We do not want any girl. Should we let girls be born so that they suffer the way we are suffering?' They say, 'what good does being alive do to us? It is better that an insufferable life ends before it can begin. It is better to go straight to heaven than stay alive and endure the kicks and blows of the world.' Are they wrong in saying this?

A backlash has begun in Punjab and Haryana. One wife to five brothers. Where will they get wives from? There is no girl in the village. The wife of the eldest brother is being used by the other brothers. There is no alternative. The Draupadi Syndrome. A tribal girl from Jharkhand, called Tripala Kumari, was taken to Haryana by a man who promised her a job there. Once there, a man called Ajmer Singh married her and asked her to go to bed with his brothers. When she refused, she was killed. There are no girls left among the Patels of Gujarat. Poor girls are now being purchased from Bihar and Orissa. They are being sold as slaves, sexual slaves and instruments for the production of sons.

The murder of girls has led to such an acute shortage of girls that an exchange system called Sata Padhyati has been initiated.

According to this system, parents agree to give their daughter in marriage on the condition that the groom's sister marries the bride's brother.

With the advent of new reproductive technology, female foeticide is now a hi-tech crime everywhere. Even in 'God's own country', Kerala. Girls are not safe anywhere. Not in the state, nor society, nor the family. The mother's womb was supposed to be the safest place. Not anymore. Now the mother's womb has become the most dangerous place for girls. As soon as it is known that it is sheltering a female foetus, the girl's safety is jeopardized. South India is also following in the footsteps of the North.

Education of girls will not prevent female foeticide. Educated girls can plan the murder of their foetuses much better than uneducated girls. Why are the educated women, who are doing fine, also committing such a crime? The reason is: lack of self-confidence. Girls have been suffering from an inferiority complex over many centuries; as a result it has permeated their flesh, bones and genes. It cannot be wiped out through conventional education. If girls are not empowered politically, socially and economically, all that so-called education can do for girls is add insult to injury, nothing more.

Nowadays men want educated wives. Girls are getting educated so that they can sell well in the marriage mart. An educated wife can do the shopping, pay the bills, look after the children's studies, and solve problems at school, all on her own. One person put it like this: 'My wife has a postgraduate degree in Maths, all the better since she can help the kids with the homework. So I don't need to engage a tutor for them. And why should my wife work outside the home? We don't need any extra money in the family. She has a lot to do at home.'

This is the lot of educated women. The money they earn is known as extra money. University degrees are meant to help the kids with their homework, nothing else. The norm is that middle class girls will not work after marriage. Girls are only supposed to keep house. Only those girls, who badly need money for survival, get permission to work outside the house.

Alas! So much for education! Educated girls have to pay more dowry. The more educated a girl is, the more educated husband she demands. And thus the amount of dowry required also escalates. Many people think that a handsome dowry enhances the dignity of the girl. However, dowry never improves the status of a girl in her in-laws' house, rather it results in loss of dignity. The more the dowry, the more the girl's status at her in-laws deteriorates. The husband is not supposed to pay dowry, no matter how educated the girl is, no matter how grand the job she holds. The 'Brides Wanted' column is clear testimony to the value of girls in this society. Wanted: A fair, beautiful, educated, homely girl from a respectable family. 'Homely girl' means a girl who will spend all 24 hours of the day on domestic chores, one who will not hold a job. 'Respectable family' means a family that will pay a handsome dowry. If the groom comes from an affluent family, it does not mean that a poor dowry will do, rather the dowry must be all the more generous. When this is the condition, why will people not believe that the birth of a girl entails huge expenses! Girls are an inferior race—this belief is ingrained in both men and women across India. And since a girl belongs to an inferior race, dowry is needed to get rid of her.

When a man marries a girl after paying money, he actually buys a slave for the household. And when a girl marries a man after paying him money, she buys for herself a status devoid of respect and dignity. Either way, there is no deliverance for girls.

The law has not been able to eradicate the dowry system. It can never be eradicated as long as every member of the family will believe that a girl cannot be as economically powerful as a boy.

Society needs a lot of change. Society must understand that girls are very important members of society, not burdens for whom dowry must be paid, not instruments for the production of sons. Self-confidence in girls is extremely needed. If women and men do not unite in the attempt to transform society, female foeticide will continue unabated.

This society is not a fit place for girls, so it is better not to allow them to be born. This logic is something like this: there is too much shouting and screaming all around, the noise pollution is giving one a headache, so it is better to chop off the head. Many claim that if women themselves choose the gender of the child before giving birth, then they will be saved from many undesired pregnancies. However, this does not cause girls to live, rather it causes them to die. How helpless she must be not to have the slightest control over the foetus growing inside her womb! Women are compelled to yield to societal as well as many kinds of family pressure and opt for abortion. An undesired pregnancy is not as terrible as this forsaken, helpless, undignified, disgraceful condition of women.

If things go on as they are now, it will not be very many decades before there will be not a single girl in the country, there will be only men. The good thing will be that men will find no more girls to torture, trample, rape and kill. Perhaps even then men will not see sense.

This disgrace is India's alone, no one else's. As long as girls will not enjoy the democratic right to be born unhindered, it will be wrong to claim that India is a democracy.

***

33

Fundamentalists are
Not to Blame at all

The other day, on seeing Nilofar Bakhtiar, a woman minister of Pakistan hugging a man, Islamist fundamentalists asked the government to sack her since hugging a man other than one's husband was anti-Islamic. The news created shock waves throughout the world. Nilofar Bakhtiar said that she did not care for such fatwas.

A few days later, a similar incident took place in India. Hollywood actor Richard Gere hugged Bollywood actress Shilpa Shetty and kissed her on the cheeks. Hindu fundamentalists started shouting that this was against Indian culture. Muslim or Hindu, no one is any less than the other. Neither of them lack religious hypocrites, self-appointed guardians of culture and anti-women people.

Once I tried to think that if Nilofar Bakhtiar and Shilpa Shetty had been men instead of women and done what they did, would there have been any problem? Would people have been up in arms crying religion and culture? Would anyone have demanded resignation of the minister? Would anybody have gone to court against them? No. It would not have been an offence if they had been men. To hug or kiss a girl—whether indigenous or foreign—is nothing but heroism in a man. We have to understand that prohibitions are meant only for women, whatever religion she may belong to, whatever be her caste, colour or class!

This religious, patriarchal society thinks that woman is the property of this society. It is the society that decides with whom a woman will mingle; with whom she will kiss; with whom she will hug; with whom she will dine; what she will wear and how; with whom she will go to bed; how many children she will give birth to; how many sons and how many daughters; under whose control she will remain; whose orders she will abide by; when she will step outside the house and when she will not; what work she will do; what she will not. A slight miss and tragedy ensues.

Women who have earned fame, become ministers or become actresses and those who are beyond the reach of the fundamentalists, cannot be crushed into oblivion. So, they are faced with waves of criticism, their effigies are burnt on the streets, processions condemning them are taken out. And the more we hear such news, the more we shudder. We forget that not-so-famous women are being indiscriminately trampled, tortured and annihilated. Since ages, they are being crushed under the bulldozer of religion, culture and the customs and traditions of patriarchy! Girls have shed a lot of tears in silent solitude. Now, many of them have forgotten how to cry. They are suffering in silence, accepting endurance to be the rule. They are dying, accepting death to be the rule.

Nilofar and Shilpa can indeed protest from their positions; for the time being, they are enjoying the protection provided by the media. But as soon as they lose their ministry or place as an actress, they are just any other girl, a, b, c, d or e. They are unsafe. Right now they enjoy the protection with the strength of which they may ignore the fundamentalists, but they enjoy that protection because they have risen to the heights of a minister or a popular actress. In the eyes of this society, height is always synonymous with masculinity. All the good qualities that are there in this world are referred to as manly. Whatever is disagreeable is womanish. Nilofar and Shilpa are enjoying the support of the people, thanks to the manly heights they have attained. The oppression they have had to face was by virtue of being women. They would have been tortured even more if they had not attained those heights. How many of those who have supported Nilofar and Shilpa extend their support to those ordinary girls who have no security to speak of?

Ordinary women have learned to think of their father and son, and even husband, as their security. But those are the people who – in the name of security – appropriate the rights of women the most. They are the ones who, in the name of security, torture women the most. They are the sentries of patriarchy. The father does not bestow that careful attention on his unwanted daughter, which he reserves for his son. The father does not give his daughter that education which will give her thorough knowledge of equal rights; that education which will make her aware of her rights as a human being; that education which will help her stand on her own feet; that education which will ensure that she will not have to dependent on somebody else. The son does exactly the same. He learns from his father, from his grandfathers, from other men in society. He learns that all women are weak, and they must be kept under control. Women must be kept under control even if they are educated, adult and self-reliant. He learns that women are to be pitied. They have to be kept alive through aid of food, clothes, medicine. He learns that a woman dedicates her life to the service of her family. It is the duty of man to pity this woman. The pity which man feels for woman is the pity people feel for the weak, the physically challenged, the infirm and infants. This pity is supposed to be 'security'. The security provided by husbands is thought to be the greatest security of a woman. But, it is at the hands of her husband that a woman is tortured the most in this world. It is the husband who rips apart a woman's rights to pieces, hacks at her liberty, keeps her imprisoned within the four walls of so-called domestic security, and makes life altogether unbearable for her through physical and mental torture.

A woman becomes an object with which the husband can do anything he wishes. She hoodwinks the law and pays dowry in order to come to the security called husband and be tortured. No part of a woman's body is hers. It is the man's. Whatever she has from head to toe belongs to men, to the husband, and the society. That is why society is enraged when a woman called Shilpa is touched or kissed on the cheeks by anybody. They believe Shilpa's breasts, belly, lower abdomen, her cheeks and lips are not her own, these are the property of society and that she has no right to make use of society's property in any way she likes, without the permission of the society. Same holds true for Nilofar too. Her breasts, belly, lower abdomen, legs, feet and head are all the property of society. A girl is born as the property of society. Nothing in her life is private; she has nothing that she can call her own.

When the fundamentalists create a furore over Nilofar and Shilpa, we are content to lay the blame on the fundamentalists and sit tight. As if, the fundamentalists are terribly evil while the rest are all extremely good. But the fault does not lie with the fundamentalists. Things are wrong at the root. The flaw lies in the society, in the structure. It is just that the fundamentalists sometimes remind us of the structure. That is all. Most people in this country see nothing wrong with this structure. It is on this structure that they build their delightful household, society.

People have written tomes on the differences among Hindu, Muslim, Buddhist, Christian, Jain, Jew and Parsee communities. But I believe that there is no real difference among them. All religions and all societies are patriarchal, and for very relevant reasons, anti-women. There are some superficial differences among the religions. Some differences may also be noted in the religious festivals, customs and practices. But the nature of all this is the same, from within they are all the same. One has to be in awe of an invisible power, keep him pleased through prayers and worship, and human society has to abide by the rule that man is the lord, woman the servant. Nowadays, highly educated women of the higher echelons of society feel irritated when they hear the word 'servant'. But I find no word that is as appropriate for women. Though they may not appear as servants at first sight, a closer look reveals that the structure of patriarchy has indeed kept women as servants—one who cannot figure this out is surely blind! Of course, women cannot but be blind. A girl who keeps her eyes wide open has no place in this society.

Whenever girls begin to open their eyes, the guardians of society become desperate to blind them. No one decries these guardians of society as fundamentalists. They are extremely respectable people. Gentlemen. Intelligent. Cultured. Fundamentalists jump about on the streets like a pack of monkeys. They behave indecently. They burn this and gut that. They are fools. Uncultured. Actually, they are less conservative than those who are gentlemen, the moderates. The fundamentalists can be easily recognized. One can be cautious about of them. They can be vanquished using a little intelligence. But the educated cannot be vanquished. Everybody thinks them to be progressive and believers in equality. They themselves think the same. It is they who, with immense shrewdness, cunning and guile, keep this male-dominated society going. They orchestrate the observation of anti-women traditions and age-old culture with even more pomp and splendour.

There are fewer effigy-burning, fatwa-issuing fundamentalists than gentlemen. This minority does not have the power to perpetuate patriarchy. Patriarchy is being kept alive by gentlemen, those who are moderates, those who are clever and cunning. Nobody will think of them as fundamentalists, but in reality they are the genuine fundamentalists. They are the ones who are doing all that needs to be done in order to keep the structure of patriarchy intact. If they had not kept patriarchy alive through the force of brains, brawn and masculinity, it would not have lived on for ages.

***

34

If People are Secured, Women too will be Safe

In comparison to all other states of India, the condition of women is better in the states of Kerala and Karnataka. A few days ago, in this better-state of Karnataka, a 46-year-old law (Shops and Business Establishment Act, 1961) was suddenly implemented. This act prohibits women from working in any sector other than hospitals and Information Technology after 8 pm. In other words, they are banned from working in night shifts. The law stipulates its violation will attract a penalty of six months' imprisonment and a fine of Rs 10,000 in cash. It was as if a bit of the Middle Ages suddenly broke loose in India like a storm.

But did the Middle Ages really storm in? Is it not true that Middle Ages openly exist in many regions and covertly almost everywhere? Has there been sufficient uplift of the mentality? The State is being labelled as democratic; some wonderful laws are also being enacted; equal rights are being assured, though not for the minority, at least for the majority community; a modern law has just been brought in to deal with domestic violence; rigid laws against casteism already exist, as do laws against the system of dowry. So what? Does not the caste system exist in society? Is not giving and taking dowry rather rampant? The girls in this country do not fall prey to this system every single day? Bride killing, rape, gang rape, trafficking of women, prostitution - all these burn like the fire of a Sati pyre, proclaiming that they live on. They care a fig for the law.

At a time when defying the Middle Ages many girls are moving towards the modernity of education and self-reliance, the Karnataka government has dug out old records and papers and, shaking off the dust from the jackets, proceeded to implement forgotten laws. The government wants to put fetters on the feet of girls. The incidence of assault on women at night is on the rise, so the solution is to put girls under house arrest. It is something like finding a solution of headache in beheading. If women are attacked during the day, then they will be prohibited from stepping outdoors in daytime as well. Is there any time when women are not under attack? Are they attacked only at night and never during the day? A girl is not safe either at night or in the day. The Karnataka government ought to find out why not. If the root cause of the problem is eliminated, the problem will no longer be there.

Although pressure from feminists has resulted in the state government keeping the matter of banning women from night shifts on hold, it should not be forgotten that an attempt had been made to issue a prohibitive order on working women. If in a state like Karnataka, women have to secure their safety by remaining confined in the house, then such a rule is bound to get ingrained in the other backward states also. The best thing for women is never to step outside the house. Then they would be perfectly safe. And, if they do indeed have to go out, extreme safety measures should be adopted. A walking prison, known as the *burqa*, should be used so as to keep them out of the sight of evil people. Thus have human beings always walked towards darkness. Thus has darkness always engulfed human beings.

But people also stride towards light. Is there nothing to illuminate the minds in this country? On the one hand, there is the triumph of Mayawati, a woman who left home and worked day and night to achieve success; on the other hand, full-fledged preparations are on to make women lame, to defeat them and make them dependent.

Just as science and religion coexist in India so do the victory and defeat of women. The sight of light and darkness warmly embracing each other causes acute apprehension. What if the cavernous mouth of darkness swallows up all light, all triumph, all science, all reason, all liberty, all equality and all humanity! The power of darkness is not negligible.

No separate laws are required to protect a woman or to protect her honour and dignity. A woman is a citizen of the state. It is the duty of the state to guarantee security to all its citizens. If the state gives security to all its citizens, then woman will automatically get all the necessary security. But does the state do that? If it had indeed done so, women would not have become victims of discrimination in government-approved laws on marriage, divorce and inheritance. If it had done so, women would have been able to go about their way on the roads and in the workplace in peace, without falling prey to violence of any kind. Women could have lived in peace and contentment in every home.

Woman is not safe anywhere. Various laws have been enacted to ensure safety, and in some places they are being implemented as well. But women are still deprived of safety in the true sense of the word. If man today refrains from attacking women, it is out of fear of the law. But the problem will really be solved only when men will refrain from attacking women out of respect for them as human beings. Not before that. Respect and esteem come from within. If it does not come from within, then whatever art or culture is artificially built by imposing from without, that is bound to collapse at a snap of the fingers.

Fear of the law is here today; it will vanish tomorrow. With time, people lose their fear. In a society ridden with corruption, ultimately no fear exists in anybody. Anybody can let loose a reign of terror with impunity. Violence against women cannot be stopped by inducing fear of law; neither can it ever do so. The only way to bring an end to this violence is to change the outlook of men. Women will never be safe in this society until man stops thinking of them as weak, as a sexual commodity, a toy, a servant, an instrument of pleasure, or a means of production.

The question is who created this outlook in men? It is created by the state, the society, the legal and the educational systems. All these systems are patriarchal and male-centric. One Mayawati can create a flutter in the realm of politics, but it is not enough to bring about a transformation in society. Society needs many more Medhas and many more Mayawatis. It needs many more people who will stand up to offer resistance. It needs many more struggles for equality.

Do women themselves have respect for women? Work it out, and the answer that will be found is 'no'. The reason is, both men and women are taught from their childhood that women are a creature of a lower category. This lesson is hammered into the heads of both men and women. It is very difficult to respect or revere a creature of lower category. That is why there is no sign of anti-women crimes abating.

The day both men and women will learn to revere and respect woman as a human being, from that day anti-women activities, anti-women laws and superstitions will cease to exist in this society. There will be then no need of frequently enacting laws for the safety of women. If women are revered, no one will rape them, no one will be involved in the trafficking of women; if they are respected, no one will push them into prostitution, no one will burn them alive.

Is there any dearth of laws against the oppression of women? How many oppressors are punished? How many women in this society enjoy safety in the true sense of the word? The symptoms are being treated rather than the disease itself. How will then the disease be cured!

If, after eight in the evening, men become uncivilized, indecent, undemocratic and inhuman, then let measures be taken to punish such men. Why women should be punished! If women are compelled to stop working in night shifts, they will be deprived of jobs. It will cause a greater harm while trying to stem another harm. And, everybody should know that if a man can be wicked after eight in the evening, he can easily be as wicked in the broad daylight. A man who is not wicked, does not become so even in the middle of the night.

Wickedness does not depend on light or darkness. It depends on outlook. Outlook depends on education. Education depends on the educational system. The educational system depends on politics. The politics of patriarchy and discrimination is now triumphing. Till men and women have faith in equality and determination to uproot discrimination, women will be compelled to live like mice—hiding into their holes at the very sight of danger. But are mice safe at all in their own burrows? Just as a meek mouse enjoys no safety, neither does a woman.

***

35

Women Should not Endure Insult

Indrani Dutta Chowdhury is a professor of English in Vidyasagar University. Her departmental head has cast his eyes on her. We know what it means. Tirthankar Das Purokayastha is hurling at her sexually loaded sentences. He does it with impunity. Who would dare to stop him? But whatever hints he dropped at Indrani, all failed. The more he fails, the more he turns into a tiger. He roars within himself and also in public. Knowing everything, people blame Indrani. Women can be blamed easily and that culture is very popular. People blame the raped instead of the rapist, claiming that her behaviourial pattern or attire or stare instigated the rapist to rape her. Blaming Indrani was similar to that. Indrani lodged compliant against Tirthankar with the vice-chancellor of the university. But got no respite. Vice-chancellor, himself a man, took the side of Tirathankar. Men take the side of the man if they face any danger. They know the character of men. If one man does not save the other, then the other will not come forward to save him when he will feel threatened. They have an unwritten agreement on this. Thus, such persons are everywhere, crowding the road to block the path of women. The women are being pushed aside.

As Indrani did not respond to his proposals, he got angry and told everyone what he said and did with Indrani. He claimed that Indrani was attracted towards him and was desperate to have relation with him. But Indrani is not a person to be defeated thus. She decided not to endure such insult. Tirthankar and his friends thought that if they assassinated her character, she will be compelled to leave the university. But that turned out to be a mirage. Indrani will not change her university and that is for the simple reason that she has not committed any wrong. It was Tirthankar who did so. If she backtracks, then the slanders will appear as true. She will then loose her peace, which is very important for an individual to retain. There is no reason for her to step back, for she knows well that she had not done anything wrong. So she has kept her head high, and is demanding punishment of the culprit.

Most men still do not consider atrocities against women, or sexual harassment, as wrong. Because it happens daily; it is too mundane, too normal and natural. Some people think when Tirthankar has not raped or attempted to rape Indrani, then why does she want him to be punished. She is doing this to make everybody understand that women are not objects to be ridiculed. Men think they have the right to utter sexually loaded words at women, but they do not have that right. They cannot do whatever they like with women.

Though the society is utterly patriarchal, in recent times some civilized laws are being imported. It has created hopes that men will be punished for their heinous acts. Men know, but most of the women do not know, that there is a law against sexual harassment. Even if they know they tolerate everything. Very few can protest.

Indrani has protested. She has filed a case against Tirthankar and I support her hundred per cent. Every woman should live with the personality and sense of dignity that Indrani has. Those males who tease women, do obscene things, they enjoy the taste of raping a woman by doing so. Women have pardoned them for long. Thus, they have given indulgence to men to be up on their heads. Now, males think being nasty with women is their birth-right. Idiotic women believe that men will be so as they have more sexual urge.

There is not an iota of truth in it. There is no sex-based difference in sexual urge. If there is, then it is that women have more of such urge. Physiology says, women have multi-orgasm power. But men have more opportunity to be nasty in this society.

This is a male-ruled society. If men should not enjoy such opportunities, who else should? Men are doing all these with those with whom they live, without whom they cannot survive. Here, they are not being wicked with one individual. They are doing it with the woman race. They can do so for they feel anything can be done with this race. This race is scared of character assassination and often they shed tears. They are beaten, and yet, they praise those very people who beat them.

When Tirthankar saw Indrani, he was carrying this set of ideas about women in his mind. That came out to prod him to do what he did. Indrani was no more a colleague, she was just a woman. He too thought like the others that she is just flesh and blood with an empty brain. That was why he could insult her so easily. He knew only men can retaliate, not women. Again, people stand by an insulted man, but not by an insulted woman. Whenever women have tried to retaliate, their well-wishers have treated that as committing excess. Instead of inspiring her, they have asked her to step back. Shouting, threatening others or showing one's strength do not behove a woman. What else could be better than this system? This patriarchal society incites men to harass women sexually with impunity.

A woman's expertise, sagacity or genius is of no value. A woman is a woman. From the Super to the sweeper, everybody makes fun of her body. Men are divided in classes—higher class and lower class. Women have but only one identity: they are women. They cannot be excused even if they belong to higher class, higher caste, the educated community or the class of genius. They are all equal. Like commodity.

This society is full of innumerable Tirthankars. If only all women were like Indrani. If they could protest! If only they had such confidence that Indrani has! If only they were not scared of those bad men, were not scared of who will say what. This world would have changed then.

***

36

Girls! When will you Live on your own Identity?

At the beginning of my stay in Calcutta, I started living in a rented house. I needed a domestic help. One of my friends was standing on the verandah, and from there she rushed towards me and said, 'Look, there goes a 'wife', you may ask her.'

I couldn't understand what she meant by the word 'wife'. So I asked her, 'Pardon, who is going there, you said?'

'A wife.' She said again.

'Is a wedding ceremony going on in the neighbourhood? Have you seen the groom as well?' I asked with curiosity. I came out on my verandah to see what the matter was. No I didn't see any sign of any wedding nearby. There was no guest, no *shehnai* and no *shamiana*. There was no trace of bride and groom. The friend was laughing aloud. It was not first of April that she would befool me. But I was there, befooled.

It took me a couple of months to come out of the riddle. It's a custom in this land to call a maid servant as 'wife' if she was married. It doesn't matter whether they know her husband or not.

'Then do you call the married men working as servants in households as husbands?' It's a bizarre question to them. But I don't think it's bizarre. Rather it's very simple, easily understandable. Yet, I fail to convince them.

The address 'wife' is not just informal or colloquial. Even in formal language this address is very much in vogue. The vernacular print media use the same language regularly. 'Wife jumps into death'; 'wife raped', 'wife murdered'; and so on. There must be pieces of news on 'wives'. But who are these 'wives'? They are women. Why are they called wives or brides? Because they are married. It means that married women are no longer women. They become wives. But men remain men even after marriage. I have not seen any news under caption, 'Husband commits suicide or husband murdered or husband raped!' In fact a woman is identified in the society not on the basis of even her gender, not by her name, not by education, not by her accomplishment, not by her talents, but on the basis of her relationship with a male.

When I go to the bazar, the fish sellers who do not know me call me *'Boudi'* (wife of elder brother). Once I asked them, 'But who is your *dada* (elder brother)?' They did not know that. They call at random all women as *boudi*. It's their common practice. Why blame the fish-walas only? All walas or hawkers indulge in the same practice. In any TV programme on cooking, the woman who demonstrates the recipes is addressed as *'boudi'*. Whoever she maybe, she must be the wife of an elder brother—this is her only identity. This habit is formed by social practice. Men have learnt from their surroundings that every woman must have a male master who is her security. They have learnt that in lieu of dowry women must live like creepers under the control of a male master. So they believe the women have no separate identity of their own.

Normally women depend on their husbands socially as well as financially. The truth is till the day they run at par with men in the fields of finance, politics and society, it will be very difficult for them to live with an identity sourced from their own beings. Until they attain physical liberty, their mental freedom will be as short lived as bubbles.

How can women possess an identity of their own if they leave their homes after marriage, live in an address belonging to somebody else, live under the control of a master and even change their name according to the name of their husbands? Their individual identity gets buried for good. What survives then is the identity based on her relationship with a man. She has to spend the rest of her life in terms of her husband's identity. I know many who boast of having accomplished a great thing by not using her husband's surname. She forgets that the surname she is using belongs to her father who is also a man. Is it not so that by using her father's surname she is submitting herself to patriarchy? We live in a society in which girls cannot marry without paying dowry which is legally prohibited. So can a woman dream of identity of her own? An identity after all cannot drop like windfall on the roads and meadows. There is no dearth of advertisements against dowry. I had a notion that a handful of uneducated and avaricious people demand dowry. But day by day, I discover how awfully wrong I am. Religion, superstition, patriarchy are so deeply engraved in the soil, the men and women are so terribly obsessed with tantra and mantra, that I am really panic-stricken now.

A few days ago Tarun Bhuian, driver of my car, asked for a lump sum of money as a loan. 'Why are you asking for money?' I had asked him.

'My sister's marriage has been settled. I need this cash for the payment of dowry.'

'Dowry! Why? It's illegal', I had said.

Tarun laughed heartily. The way he laughed, it seemed he wanted to mean that he had not seen a fool like me before.

'Dowry illegal! Since when? It's going on as smartly as before,' Tarun went on. He admitted naively that he had also taken dowry both in cash and kind Rs 80,000, a colour TV set, a refrigerator, furniture and of course ornaments. The groom they had chosen for his sister is a lawyer.

'Even a lawyer demands dowry? I asked in amazement.

'Of course.' Replied Tarun with a smile. 'They have made some concession because my sister is handsome.'

'A lawyer bridegroom is not poor. So why had he asked for money.'

'He is asking for money because it is the convention.'

I tried to convince Tarun: 'Look, instead of spending two lakhs for your sister's marriage, I would suggest you to spend that amount for her higher education. She will appear in HS Exam. Is it the time for her to get married? Why don't you make her a lawyer instead? Then you will not have to pay dowry. You're sending her off to a stranger's house. You don't know how her life shall be there—perhaps she will be tortured, battered and then driven out of home. Then she will have to take refuge in your home. That is also degrading, humiliating. There will be no end to her ordeals. So I suggest you to let her continue with her education, then stand on her own feet. Then she need not look up to any boy's compassion. She can live with her head held high.'

This time Tarun laughed louder than before. Perhaps he meant that he had not seen anybody more impractical than me.

'Are you sure', I went on. 'Your sister is willing to give up her studies?'

'Now it depends on her in-laws. If they like it she can, but if they don't she can't.' Replied Tarun.

'Oh, your sister has no say here?'

Tarun laughed once again, 'How can that be? She is a woman after all.'

Remaining silent for quite sometime I said, 'It means she will become the property of her husband and in-laws, right?'

Tarun with a mouthful of smile replied, 'Of course she will be, for it's the usual practice.'

Tarun's countenance revealed that he was pitying me for my lack of knowledge about prevailing social customs.

So, some days later, Tarun's sister will begin her life as somebody's wife, somebody's sister-in-law, somebody's aunt and so on. Her individual and original identity shall be lost. In this way, girls like Tarun's sister are daily being threatened with extinction. Instead of building a self-identity of their own, they are courting self immolation in the fire of patriarchy. Burning out all of their prospects, they choose the life of a creeper. This is not at all a life worth living.

***

37

Who is Guilty?
Men or Patriarchy?

"Male domination is so rooted in our collective unconscious that we no longer even see it. It is so in tune with our expectations that it becomes hard to challenge it. Now, more than ever, it is crucial that we work to dissolve the apparently obvious and explore the symbolic structures of the androcentric unconscious that still exists in men and women alike."

Pierre Bourdieu

The other day I was invited to a programme on Kolkata TV. The programme presented a freshly collated bunch of recent comments made by poets, writers and ordinary readers about me. The first comment was from Nabaneeta Deb Sen. I am a fan of Nabaneeta, particularly of her sense of humour. A few days ago, we returned to Kolkata together after participating in a feminist programme in Delhi. That journey of ours was replete with erudition, and also brimful of humour. Time had simply flown. Nabaneeta often said that she liked my writings, especially the ones criticizing patriarchy. I remember I had read out to her a piece I had written and she had praised it to the skies sitting in my house. While commenting on me in Kolkata TV, I found this same Nabaneeta saying: "The difference between 'Taslima and ourselves is that we are against patriarchy, she is not. That is to say, we criticize the system, but with Taslima, it is different, she does not do that, she is not against patriarchy, she is a misandrist." The comment left me speechless for quite some time. For the past two decades, I have criticized religion, fundamentalism and patriarchy, standing firmly in favour of women's rights. I have written numerous books on the subject; for this very reason, I have been exiled from my own country for more than an age now, and this is what I get in return from a revered feminist intellectual! What a cruel joke she has cracked on my life!

I do not believe that Nabaneeta Deb Sen has not read any of my books. Not that there is any dearth of people who pass comments without having read any book or article. But why should I cast her in that group! She is a responsible person. When she has put forward her view, she has surely not done so like an irresponsible person. I know that those who make comments of this kind are invariably people who have not read my writings, or, even if they have read it, failed to understand a word. They do this in Bangladesh, they do this in West Bengal too. But never before I earned such calumny from a writer of Nabaneeta Deb Sen's stature. It is a lot like character assassination. If I do not remain respectful to my humanist ideals and principles, if I suffer the loss of honesty to speak the truth, I myself will admit that I have no character. But if I am labelled as something I am not, then what is it other than character assassination! The way I define it, the adjective 'characterless' has no association with sexuality, rather it is all about deceit, lowliness, dishonesty, lies, deception, slyness and pretence.

Nabaneeta Deb Sen and I were guests at two programmes on the Parampara slot of ETV. Many other poets, writers and artists also featured on Parampara and their programmes are already aired. But for some mysterious reason, the two programmes on the Nabaneeta Taslima duo have not been telecast till date, though a year has gone by since the shoot. On the sets of the show, I had wanted to know why a woman of personality like Nabaneeta Deb Sen used her husband's surname. I had also wanted to know why I had no right to join her woman writers' organisation called Soi when almost every other woman writer did. Both the programmes were pretty scholarly, feminist programmes. But nowadays, officials of established institutions are inclined to choose feminists for hacking.

For a long time now, I am criticizing religion and patriarchy in my writings and speeches. This is because I believe in human rights. And since I believe in human rights, I believe in the rights of women. To me, 'human' includes both man and woman. As women are persecuted in society because they are women, as they are being oppressed, as numerous patriarchal conspiracies stand in the way of achievement of liberty and equal rights by women, so I protest against those anti-women rules and regulations and cunning, complex conspiracies. And because I do so, some call me a feminist and some call me a humanist. Idiots happily maintain that I am a misandrist.

The word 'misandrist' is dangerous. It can smear someone well. People go up in arms. They shower you with hatred. Those who want to keep women under male subjugation are ready to devour me whole. If they cannot do so, they do something very akin to it, and that is slander me as a 'misandrist'. I have been a victim of slander for a very long time. Both fundamentalists and others spit at me in hate. 'She knows nothing about literature, she just wants publicity': such delectable bits of disparagement have been floating in the air like virus. In this way, the politics to belittle my fight for equality and truth in the eyes of people goes on. There is nothing new about it.

'Men are good, patriarchy is bad'. Everybody says this straightaway, making no bones about it. It all sounds wonderful. But I have a question, to everybody and to me too, whether patriarchy has dropped from the sky. Patriarchy is an ism in which the laws are in favour of men, the social and familial rules and regulations are in favour of men, just about everything in this world and society is in favour of men; everything is male-centric. No, this ism has not dropped from the sky, it has been created by men. They take every advantage of this ism. The role of most women is to help men enjoy it. I am a critic of patriarchy, but I cannot claim that man is not the father of patriarchy. When I speak, I have to speak the truth and this is it. While we boast of our civilization, there lives on a savage, uncivilized custom called patriarchy, and it thrives side by side with developed technology and a whole host of spectacular achievements in the fields of art, culture, philosophy and science. Who is keeping it alive? Air? No, it is not air, truth to tell, it is men. And also women. To be a female is not to be a feminist. I have seen a large number of men who are greater feminists than many feminists. I have also seen a large number of women who are ardent flag bearers and patrons of patriarchy.

There have been quite a few movements for equality the world over. Thanks to these movements, many ancient customs that perpetuated discrimination have been eliminated. But till date patriarchy has been left unscathed. What do you think is the reason? Is it that this patriarchy has tumbled down from the sky and is made of iron? Or is it because people try with all their might to keep it alive? Is it or isn't it wrong to blame those who do so? Since patriarchy is an anti-woman custom, since the contradiction between women's rights and patriarchy goes back to the beginning of time, so while speaking of human rights, I have to speak of patriarchy and those who are keeping this ism alive. If I don't, I'll be guilty of practising double standards. I have to bring to light the forces which stand opposed to women's liberty.

Patriarchy is bad, men are good – this is just like saying, capitalism is bad but capitalists are good. If I had not been slandered as a misandrist, then maybe I would have continued to criticize patriarchy the way I have always done. I would not have tried to identify its organizers and leaders. Those who keep the organizers happy through pampering and indulgence while hurling brickbats at the ism, do they not know that an ism has no body, no sense or brains of its own? That an ism cannot talk? That ism does not control ism, human beings control it! Don't they know that brickbats notwithstanding, an ism will continue to remain in sound form if those who control the ism are left unharmed. If they are turned all the more active by oiling the machinery, then the day is not far when the triumph of patriarchy will bring on the ruin of the world!

I suspect that those who vent their anger only on the system, while forgiving those who build and protect this system, actually want—underneath their cunning—male domination and exploitation to be perpetuated.

No, I am not a misandrist, I never was. I have not entered this struggle out of anger towards any individual man or out of personal hatred for men. Among the men are my lovers, my dear friends, sympathizers, comrades-in-arms. I just want to identify those men who will let nothing change in this rotten old patriarchal society, who will not alter their anti-women attitudes even at the slightest bit, those who do not believe in equality of men and women, those who pamper patriarchy, those who have sworn to trample women underfoot all their lives. I want them to grow into sensible human beings. I also want those women to grow into sensible human beings who consciously do all they can to keep patriarchy alive. I want them to reject gender-based discrimination; I want them to believe in truth and equality with all their heart. If one believes in humanism, if one practises humanism as a way of life, then there remains no distinction between the rights of women and men.

***

38

Why are Girls Reluctant to Use
Law on Domestic Violence?

Bhasvar Chattopadhyay, Rudraneel Ghosh, Sanjay
Mukhopadhyay, Krishnakishore Bhattacharya and Suman
Bhattacharya—they are all associated with art and culture.
However, that does not mean they do not belong to this society,
a male-dominated society. It is believed that those men who
sing, write poetry, play musical instruments, are actors—in
other words, those men who belong to the world of art and
literary—are noble human beings with faith in humanity,
human rights and women's liberty. This is one hundred per
cent wrong. The magnitude of goodness or badness present in
those outside the world of art and literature is equal to those
present inside the said world. An illiterate peasant from a village
may believe in women's liberty, but a famous actor may not.
There is no difference between the educated and the uneducated
on the question of women's rights. Rather, it is seen that the

patriarchal attitude is comparatively more pronounced among the educated. This is because the educated are better equipped to learn the mantra. They can learn the rules and regulations, and the details of patriarchy perfectly. The uneducated mass cannot learn it so perfectly.

Whether it is men, who are peasants, petty workers in some petty job, or men holding grand positions in large establishments, or for that matter professionals like lawyers, judges, doctors, engineers, scientists, industrialists, artists, writers or whatever; whether they are rich or poor, educated or uneducated, it is seen that all of them are almost equally skilled in oppressing women. Regardless of how much wealth they possess, they all live in the same society, a society which is patriarchal, a society which runs on the basis of male rules, male supremacy and continuance of the male family line. The educated do not lag behind when it comes to oppressing women. It is absolutely wrong to think that an educated person will necessarily accord respect to women. There is no contradiction between patriarchy and the conventional education girls and boys receive in school, college and university. Our children do not read a word against patriarchy in any book in the school. Textbooks contain nothing that will propagate knowledge in favour of equal rights for women. Conventional education renders every possible help to ensure that students grow up with a patriarchal attitude. Looking within the house and without, children see and understand that a woman's place is in the house, as homemaker, as caregiver, as attendant to the husband; while a man dwells in the vast, boundless world outside, in learning, in science, in wealth, in rebellion, in revolution, in malevolence, in triumph. A woman may be learned or illiterate, rich or poor, may live in the town or in the country, in each case she is equally helpless before the anti-women culture of a patriarchal society.

Nobody is unaware of this. No one with a bit of sense will argue on this. But I see some educated men in Kolkata say that the law on domestic violence is not suitable for everybody in India. When asked why, they reply rather gravely that a law which works for a girl living in a village in Murshidabad does not work for a girl living in a multi-storey flat in Gariahat. When asked why it does not work for the latter, it is argued that the educated and urban girls are not tortured the way uneducated rural girls are. 'Even when village women are beaten unconscious, they do not rush to file a case; but educated urban women have to be but touched and they start brandishing Section 498.' I stared at the gentleman open-mouthed for some time. Before I could come out of the daze, he prattled that women were greatly misusing this law. "His law is a law against men. If a girl is beaten up she can file a diary at the police station. But why 498? This law is being used to harass scores of innocent men. Urban males have now figured it all out. Which is why there is a backlash," he said his eyes burning with anger, radiating hatred for women.

I am constantly reminded of a government survey: two-thirds of married women in India are victims of domestic violence. I badly want to know how many of these women have filed cases of domestic violence against their husbands and in-laws. I am not aware of the figure. But I can well imagine that out of a lakh or more oppressed girls, maybe one takes recourse to the law. Those who do not go to court have a number of reasons for not doing so. These reasons may be that they do not know that there exists any law against domestic violence; that they are financially dependent on their husbands; that if a woman files a case against her husband, he will stop supporting her or throw her out of the house. Girls agonize over where they will go in such a case, what they will eat, what they will wear, etc. Even if the girl herself earns, she is apprehensive that if she gets a divorce, her own income may not allow her to lead a comfortable life. She also is in constant fear that people will say she is not a decent girl and if there is a divorce, the kids' future always worry her.

Women also live with a hope that their husbands' attitude may change in the future and that she should wait for that. Female in a divorce has no end of trouble in this society. She worries that the divorce will make her life unbearable and if she marries another man, he too may be of the same kind. The negativity in her makes her believe that the society is like that. So many other women are sailing in the same boat. If they can take it lying down, why can't she! People at her parents' house advise her to settle for a compromise rather than go to court. They tell her God has made this match, so to break it is to sin against God.

Generally, fear and domestic violence are the main reasons of not filing a case of domestic violence against an oppressive husband. It is not difficult to guess that men are hopping mad with those girls who have overcome fear and hesitation to file cases of domestic violence.

The law on domestic violence is not a law in favour of women and against men. It is a law against injustice, torture, oppression, etc. Women are being oppressed all the time. Women have to suffer because they are physically, mentally, socially and economically weak. Who stands in the way of their becoming strong? It is not as if we don't know.

The societal system is such that in this male-dominated society men have appeared in the role of masters, while women are in the role of servants. The word 'servant' is harsh on the ear; but even if one says 'mistress' instead of 'servant' there would be no reversal of role for women. The status accorded to women in patriarchal society in ancient times has been zealously maintained till date. The position of women has not changed. Even now, women have to move from their own or their father's house to the husband or to the in-laws' place after marriage.

Women who fight in the court do not get any money out of it, neither is it beneficial to them on any count. Women, and not men, are ostracized for fighting this case. Men are wary of entering into relationships with women involved in a case of this kind. So when a woman files such a case despite all the risks, it is because she has no option. Women file this case in order to save their lives, to salvage their honour and prestige. They save themselves from a daily dose of unbearable humiliation, unspeakable neglect and even tragic death. No one with self-confidence and self-respect wishes for an existence that entails getting beaten up everyday. Particularly when the person who beats is supposed to be one's best friend in the journey of life, one's greatest sympathizer.

Men are against the law on domestic violence, because this law comes in the way of doing whatever one likes with one's wife. A man's wife is his own conquered possession—if one cannot keep one's own possession under control with kicks and prods, sticks and staves, blows and bashes, then whom can one keep under control! If he cannot rape her when she is unwilling to have sex, then his manliness is not worth speaking of! This law has hit out at the machismo of men. That is why they want urban, educated women to be like the poor, illiterate, oppressed women of villages. They too should bear all injustice in silence. Men get angry if women do not show endurance. They get really incensed.

Men do not want women to understand the meaning of liberty and be conscious of their rights. They do not want women to have any sense of self-respect. That is why they, cunningly, put forward the charge of misuse of this law, and thereby speak against the law.

This is nothing new. In all countries of the world, men opposed to the women's rights have seethed with anger, shouted in protest whenever any law has been enacted against male injustice and oppression on women. And, these were all kinds of men; rather there were more urban, supposedly educated men, than toiling peasants.

Whenever any woman tries to straighten her back bent with beatings, hold her head high and swear that she will not be beaten ever again, men immediately point their fingers at her and brand her as a bad woman, a fallen girl. There is nothing new in this. This has happened in all countries, in all societies. It continues to happen.

Two-thirds of married women in India are oppressed by their husbands. The day every oppressed woman, that is each of the two-thirds of married women, sends her oppressor husband to jail on the charge of domestic violence, that day I shall know that women in India have acquired a certain level, however slight it may be, of consciousness; that they have some, however little, amount of self-respect. The day their fear fades away, their hesitation disappears, that day I shall know that women have become capable of standing with their heads held high. If one has self-respect, one can always find some way of becoming self-reliant.

We should not forget that women are not as much tortured, as much humiliated, as much dishonoured by anybody as they are by their own husbands. We should not forget that more women are murdered by their husbands than by anyone else. We should not forget that in the maximum number of cases it is the husband who drives a woman to suicide.

***

39

Tapasi: Had there been no Politics Behind it

Men have raped and then burnt alive a 15-year-old girl. This is the incident. Everybody knows it. They know about it because it is linked with politics and political persons. The accused rapist, and he is the killer too, is arrested after investigation, and that has found its place in 'breaking news' items of TV channels and on the front pages of newspapers. A furore is going on about who are being arrested and with which party they are affiliated to.

I wonder what would have happened if this girl Tapasi Malik's rape and murder was not related to politics, if political persons were not involved in it! Would there have been so much hullabaloo about it? Would there be a CBI enquiry? Would anyone have ever been caught?

Tapasi Malik belonged to a very poor family. There are lakhs of such poor girls in this state of West Bengal. No one bothers about what they eat, what they wear, whether they have any land or whether they manage to earn a living. No one is interested to know whether they are being kicked or beaten with a broom, whether they are being insulted, being raped in daylight or in the dark of night. Lakhs of girls like Tapasi shed their tears in private.

There is no reason to assume that the women of this country spend their lives without being raped. There is no reason to assume that the women of this country or this state enjoy all their rights in every walk of life, and any unfortunate incident of rape creates a furore.

If two political parties were not involved in it–one in the incident and the other in demanding conviction of the culprits—and if they were not opposed to each other, this rape and killing would have been treated as insignificant news, or no news at all, just like daily incidents of rape and murder. In India, a huge number of women are being sold, being trafficked, being duped, and being compelled to take up prostitution every day and a very large number of women are falling victim to rape, murder and suicide every day in India. Tens of thousands of women are victims of poverty, injustice, lack of education and ill-health. No one considers this the most important, or even a major problem. All powerful men, whether they are in politics or in something else, nurture a set idea about women that the males belong to the ruling class and the females to the subject class. Not only subjects, they are subjects of low caste. The day Tapasi's murderer was caught and people came to know that Tapasi had not committed suicide, but was raped and then killed, that day a powerful man of the city made faces and said, "Crap, is Tapasi an object to be raped! If I were given seven hundred crores, I would not have been able to rape her. Did her appearance have anything to be roused?" When I heard this, I wondered whether this was playing only in the mind of this famous man, or many other men shared this. I believe, many others did.

Men do not get pained by the heart-rending news of rape and killing of a woman; rather they enjoy it by imagining themselves as the rapist, and then they relish the murder. This happens in their mind, and that is why the sorrow they express outwardly looks artificial. Otherwise, so many rapes could not be committed.

Most of the news of rapes does not come into open. Those are kept secret. Seventy per cent of incidents of rape are not registered. According to government estimates, every hour a woman is raped in India.

Why the males rape the females? Because they have physical strength, and the greatest strength is that of being a male. In the past, rape was not considered a crime. Now, from the legal point of view it is a crime. But it is not considered so by society. As society does not consider it a crime, so the rapists can move about freely, but the raped woman has to hide her face. The rapist need not be ashamed of his act, but the raped should be, this is societal law. So, most of the raped persons do not go to court, and no man, even the rapist, wants to marry her. The raped person faces sanctions from society. Not the rapists. People do not rally by the victim, but behind the perpetrator of the crime. In this society, there is an inseparable link between the tormentor and power. The tradition of being attracted towards and pledging loyalty to power is very much living even today.

256 Taslima Nasreen No Country for Women

Those who raped Tapasi and those who planned it are now being found out. What would have happened if no political party or powerful people had demanded CBI investigation? No one would have been caught. If the powerful did not come out to raise demand for bringing to book Dhananjoy*, would anything have happened to him? In this cruel rapist-dominated society women are only silent spectators. The male-folk plough the female-land and prove their manhood by showering it with their semen and by raping it. People stand by the raped person not for her, but to further their own interest. If the raped person is killed, it gives them better opportunity to raise various demands. Does any political party care to organise a procession for the raped woman who has not been killed? Only death may give to a raped person; but not always, only in those cases where power or politics is involved.

Tapasi is a wretchedly poor girl. Anyone could have raped her and burnt her alive. Why should anyone have to say anything about it? They said that she went out with a jar of kerosene. So they would have claimed she committed suicide by pouring kerosene all over her body. Her relatives and neighbours would have believed it. People in general would have known that suffering from want and diseases, she burned herself to death, just like other hundreds of Tapasis.

The furore over Tapasi's death has nothing to do with Tapasi. Some days later, people will forget who Tapasi was. Like that famous man, some others will remember that she was ugly, so

---

* Dhanonjay was hanged for raping and killing a girl in whose apartment he worked as a security staff.

ugly that even the thought of raping her would not have crossed their minds.

Women should wear so much beauty that men should feel like falling in love. Men want women should have such beauty that induces in their mind a will to rape them. Otherwise there would be disaster. Even after death, a woman would be target of banter. Tapasi's death has saved her. At least, she has got some compassion. If she were only raped, and not killed, people would have said that she herself instigated Debu to rape her. She was raped because she sat to answer nature's call. Had she not done that she would not have been raped.

What difference it makes for such poor women whether they are raped or not. They are raped everyday, killed everyday by that society that nurtures inequality. She would have been married to someone like Debu and would have been tortured all through her life. She could have been sold, or trafficked, might have to spend her life in a dark dungeon of a brothel. What else could be the fate of a hapless rural girl? In West Bengal, young women are falling victims to trafficking in such a way that in many villages there are not even one of them left. They are enticed by the promises of job or marriage, and then they are sold to brothels in various parts of the country. There they are raped everyday, and bear a little less pain than being burned alive.

The suicide rate of young women is more in India than in any other country of the world. Why do they do this? Has anyone tried to find out? Why are they compelled to commit suicide? Why do they die so young? And how many of this increasing number of suicides are really suicides, and how many are murders? Who knows? Who is interested to know?

If the rapist is brought to book only if it involves politics, then that is not justice. That is tantamount to giving someone extra advantage, or put someone at disadvantageous position. That trial is real trial which is not done under pressure of the rich or the powerful, but is spontaneous. If the punishment of the poor who rapes a rich girl and the rich who rapes a poor girl get is the same that is fair trial.

***

40

Suicidal Women

I have been writing for long about the rights and freedom of women. Once, I enquired about the reactions to my writings. I was told that women have criticized me the most. 'For whom I steal, she says I am a thief.' No, for me even this unfortunate piece of information is not something new.

Many people have told me, "Write about the faults of women also." Amusingly, women have said this.

"What is the fault of the women?" I asked.

"Don't find any fault with them?" the women are amazed.

I heave a sigh: "What is the fault of the victims?"

I have to write about the faults of the victims. Both men and women are insisting that I should write about the faults of women. The maximum applaud I got was for the piece that I wrote sometime back criticizing Nabanita Debsen. I cannot differentiate between those men and women who want me to write about women's faults. They speak the same language. When women represent men, appear in the role of supporter and saviour of patriarchy, then men and women cannot be differentiated. At times, I feel patriarchy would not have survived only by the conspiracy of men or by the intellect and power of men, unless it got so much help and cooperation from women.

I hear of quarrel between the mothers-in-law and the daughters-in-law only in this Indian subcontinent. In the society where women do not live in their in-law's; where women are economically independent; where they do not fall victims of gender discrimination; there the daughters-in-law and mothers-in-law do not quarrel.

Behind such quarrels, dependence on others and patriarchy have a big role. Here the practice is that the women will live in her husband's or in the in-law's house after marriage. In the in-law's, her husband's relatives, like the father-in-law or mother-in-law do represent her husband. Whoever represents a male, be a big one or a tiny one, all are powerful. If the son fails to serve patriarchy properly, the mother takes up the responsibility. The daughter-in-law is a slave, and she has to start with playing that role. If she does well in this role, she will become a representative. In some families, the son selects his wife as his representative, and in those families the mother-in-law does not live happily. The quarrel centres on the point of who has more rights over the male. In those societies where gender discrimination does not exist, there no one fights on this. Because there the value of a male and that of a female are the same. Those women who are dependent on someone else, they vie for the major share of his compassion by entertaining him. They do so because they are dependent on him.

No one condemns jealousy between the brothers, quarrels between son-in-law and father-in-law, the strife between the brothers-in-law, the fight between the uncle and nephew. But a little argument between the women is condemned by everybody. As though the women are aliens. We will throw them in muck, but they must remain pure.

The high profile quarrel between women (between mother-in-law and daughter-in-law) is a variation of professional jealousy. Their profession is dependence on the others, and they live by doing that. Who are pressurizing the women to adopt dependence on the others as their profession? It is patriarchy. Who made this patriarchy? Men made this. This is also behind the quarrel between mothers-in-law and daughters-in-law. But if jealousy is to be there, let it be among self-dependent women to go up the ladder by overtaking each other. Even better, if it is for overtaking the men.

If women are not self-dependent, they would bicker with each other. Women live below the men and so they fight more with each other. This is a constant fight between those who are in favour of patriarchy and those who criticise it. This squabble is not between the women, this is between men and women. A group of women are in favour of women's rights, the other against it. One group is with men, the other with women.

'Women are enemies of women'—this adage is formed by men. They contributed heavily to popularize it. Are not men enemies of men? If we count among whom the enmity is more, definitely it is hundred times more among the men than among the women.

If a woman speaks out against another, men are pleased. They consider that woman prudent and intelligent. They enjoy when a woman criticizes another for her skimpy clothes, her relation with men. Because it is basically their speeches that they hear from the mouths of the women. Those women were brought up with their mentality, they are their copies. Female copies. It gives men more pleasure to see their female copies. If a man condemns a woman, they cannot relish that much. When women do that, for men it is tantamount to sexual pleasure.

A popular allegation is that the maids are tortured more by the women than the men. When men torture them, not much is said about it. If women do it, then it is condemned. Women are controlled by the others. They cannot control much. So they try to control someone below them. Like the maid. They get a sort of satisfaction out of it. They can then feel that they too are taller than some others. It is all the same if in place of a maid there is a male domestic help. If a woman's husband feels like raping the maid, she tortures the maid and not the husband. Here too she beats the weak one, and not the stronger one. Thus, she gets rid of her pain. They still have not acquired enough strength to take on the powerful.

Women have so long been given epithets like shy, illusory, compassionate and loving, that people have forgotten that they too are made of flesh and blood. Women may not be so much bellicose, envious, revengeful, narrow-minded, wicked, cruel, ferocious, lowly, indecent like the men-folk, but they can have a part of it. Have not they learned anything even after cohabiting with the men for so long? The way the males beat to death a pickpocket, women cannot do that. But it is not so that women can do nothing.

Why people get scared when they confront cruelty of women. Because it is expected that women should in their behaviour follow their image, that they are kind. With this image ingrained in the head, cruelty is totally unexpected. So one can tolerate cruelty of the males, but not of the females.

The struggle for freedom and equality of women is a fight for an ideology. Women may believe in it and men may not. The opposite also happens. Some women may not have faith in it while some men may. (Very few men believe in women's lib, and fewer participate actively in the struggle). It is related to women, but this is not a gender issue, it is a matter of ideology. So, if all women have not liked my writings on women's rights, there is no element of surprise in that. This patriarchal society is not so idiotic that it will make all the women conscious about women's liberation so that they all support it. After being dependent on others for too long, women think this is their safe shelter, and they are satisfied with the little light that comes through the holes of the prison they are in.

I want complete freedom of men, and that seems too much to many women. At times, men understand better what I say about women's liberation. Because they have enjoyed freedom and they know the meaning of it. Men oppose me, because they know what I am targeting them. Women oppose me as they do not get what I try to convey. Both oppose me in the same language, but for different reasons.

Women are victims of patriarchy. But, it is also true that women kill themselves. If today women were conscious about their rights, could organise them to overcome the crisis of identity, if the bond between them turned stronger, had they felt for and respected each other, if they were sincere in cooperation and stood by each other for empowerment of women, then the patriarchy could not withstand it. The world would have been much better place to live.

***

41

Only Wife or Fiancée?

Two Bengali films have got tremendous response in this city. Advertisements of the films are everywhere. People are writing on them. The directors and actors are being interviewed. By incorporating English dialogues liberally, it is made explicit that these films are for educated and conscious people, for people having a modern mind, and for the new generation with new outlook. These new-generation boys and girls say five sentences in English along with one sentence in Bengali. Upper class fellows are marked by their bad pronunciation of Bengali language. We cannot deny that this is the way of young modern citizens.

In the film *Anuranan* (Reverberation), two characters—Rahul and Amit—reflect this trend. They are busy with their work. One is an architect, the other a businessman. Their wives are very smart, educated women. What do they do? They are 'housewives'. Parasites. Their work is limited to dressing up, wearing good outfits, giving company to their husbands and wandering about.

In *Anuranan*, one man develops a relation with the other man's wife. The man is Rahul, and the wife of the other man is Preeti. Preti is one who does not enjoy her husband's love, not even get her husband to mitigate her physical need. Rejected by her husband, she is attracted towards another man. Her eyes and her smiles reflect covert indulgence. That is only natural as her husband cannot provide her happiness of any kind, mental or physical. Her wave-length matches not with her husband, but with her husband's friend. They have a lot of common ground. Rahul is now in the hills, and she easily goes to the distant hills to her friend. There is nothing to assume that this relationship will not develop into love. Such a sequence is created that if the man touches her, she will almost swoon.

A weak screenplay is always marked by its attempts to surprise the viewers. It goes very close to a situation where one should say 'I love you', but they do not say that; likely to sleep together, but not doing that. In the night, when they go to their separate rooms, the girl looks back from the door with thirsty eyes. It seems that they will not get inside their separate rooms, but will share a single room, but even that does not happen. Well, if not on that night, they will share a room another night—there remains limitless possibility of that. It is easy surmise that the relationship is not of plain friendship as Rahul has not revealed to his beloved wife Nandita, whom he calls with or without any reason, that Preeti has arrived at his place. While on her way to the hills, or even after reaching there, Preeti too has not told Nandita that she was going to Rahul or has come to Rahul. Keeping in mind the rumours, and the hatred Preeti had received, nothing was unexpected. It is not new in Indian cinema that wives forgive their husbands who get involved with another woman or indulge in sexual relation. The wives look at them with forgiving eyes and adore them. (In *Anuranan*, the adoration comes in a different way: as the husband was not alive, so Nandita adores her husband by adoring her husband's friend or would-be lover).

For a long time, such stories are being made. In simpler terms, these are just cultural movements to make polygamy of the male acceptable to society. Earlier, Rituparno Ghosh has made *Dosar*. Nowadays, it has become a little tough to make these things easily acceptable, so one has to die. In *Dosar*, the woman dies; in *Anuranan*, the man dies. If someone dies in a film, the viewers turn sympathetic to him and so it becomes easier to manage the extramarital affair. Nowadays, modernism is reflected by a little dose of anger on the part of the wives before they adore their husbands again. What else the women who are dependent on the others can do? The male directors are now making films with huge money and intellect to create minds that will accept more profoundly the extramarital love and sexuality of the men. They are getting applause for that.

In comparison to *Anuranan*, the backdrop of the story in *Bong Connection* is better. But the film is marred by unreal theme and too much of story. Here also, the same thing happens. Arup and Andy are the two main male characters. One goes to a foreign country to build up a carrier in computer science or information technology, and we see how busy he is there. The other person comes to India from a foreign land and gets busy in his passionate work on music. And what are the chores of the two main female characters? They become friends or fiancées of the men. When the men get some time after their hard work, the women give them company and pure joy. Both of the female characters are young, attractive, they sport fashionable clothes and are fluent in English. But they have a single identity, a single role: they are lovers of the men. Those men are busy with important works, and the women are busy in winning their minds, to build them up to be creepers dependent on men.

These are the traditional roles of men and women in Indian films. But when a film boasts of reflecting the new time and modernity, an expectation is created that in it women too will be shown as modern women, as bold, independent, conscious human being with fighting spirit. But, alas! The films that are known as reflections of old patriarchal values are not so fearsome as these made by famous directors that boast of modernity, packaged as modern but at core very traditional. They have revolutionized the definition of modernity.

In this society, modernism denotes only the attire, the dialogues. How much they boast of modernity, there is not an iota of modernity in them. They show fashionable lives of young men and women, but the mentality of those characters remains traditional. Modernism is not to be found in attire or words. It exists in intellect, in mentality, in the brains. In realization, in conscience, in wisdom. In *Bong Connection*, the women are busy in serving food and men. But what about the younger people? They too are following, or are compelled to follow the same trend.

It is quite natural that non-homosexual men and women will be attracted towards the other sex. It is normal to develop friendship, love and relation between two such persons. But, if one has to sacrifice one's self for that, then it is not a healthy relation. In a healthy relation, one is not of less value as a human being than the other; one does not enjoy more rights than the other; no one is dependent financially on the other. If dependence is there, then one goes up and the other down. Then one is powerful, the other powerless. Then there will be grievances and compromises.

Our literature and art is patronizing patriarchy throughout all ages. For how long the artists and writers will claim them as modern after muzzling the rights of women and making them sheer commodity. At one point of time idiocy comes to an end. Only in this subcontinent its reign never ends.

***

42

On Sexual Harassment

The news was like this: 'The pregnant wife served meal to her husband Aker Sheik. He noticed a hair in the rice. In rage he got up and holding his wife's tuft of hair started beating her. Then he poured kerosene all over her body and burnt his wife Jyotsnabibi to death.'

It happened in a village in Murshidabad. Hearing this news, some of my acquaintances commented: "Muslims are not human beings. Only they can do such heinous things." I did not remind them of Tapasi Malik episode. I referred to another news published the same day: 'Sumana Basu did not comply with her lover Abhishek Chowdhury, and so the youth slashed the throat of his beloved with a razor.' I tried to convince these people that it had nothing to with Hindus or Muslims. It was a case of gender discrimination. The mindset to look upon women as slaves and sex objects is at the root of all these. It is common in all religious communities to humiliate, ignore, heckle and neglect women.

My acquaintances departed. I do not know how far I was able to convince them that day. Had they been in that bus, they would have, I suppose, behaved like others in the bus; they would have silently witnessed the incident without saying anything. I am talking about that bus in which a girl was sexually abused by two youths. Nobody had protested except two fellows Jagannath and Subhendu. Then the two ruffians, accompanied by four others travelling in the same bus, brutally thrashed Jagannath and Subhendu. When they were being beaten, none of the passengers came forward. They were silent even when the conductor threw all the six out of the bus. The passengers knew quite well that the duo's life was at stake.

In this subcontinent, sexual harassment is termed eve-teasing. It is a dexterous attempt to romanticize an awfully ugly thing like sexual harassment and lighten the degree of terror and uncouthness. Making an allusion to the romantic pair Adam-Eve, teasing is looked upon as something very harmless and romantic. That's why in Indian cinemas men are depicted as heroes when they chase the heroine, whistle, blink one eye and tease them before they enter into a romantic relation with them and take part in duet songs and dances to purely entertain crores of Indian audience. Hence sexual harassment can never be viewed as a crime in India. The boys sexually harass girls because they do not see anything wrong in it. When passengers barring a few exceptions do not protest, the criminals turn more reckless and get further impetus to carry on. Everyone knows that keeping mum in a situation like this is as good as supporting it.

Gentlemen are feigning astonishment on why none in the bus rose in protest. I believe the male passengers did not protest because they were relishing the act. The female passengers were silent because they feared to be heckled if they had come out in protest. They were sure that no one would come forward to stand beside them if they were heckled like that poor girl.

The reward of protest is good thrashing. No one utters a single word against it. I do not agree that it is due to lack of courage. In several fields, people are showing courage. They are indulging in corruption; queuing up at brothels at Sonagachi; heedless of the consequences, pouncing upon someone else's wife; sexually abusing young girls—all these acts require guts which they never lack. Despite knowing that the offences like domestic violence, human trafficking, gang-rape, child rape, sexual abuse are punishable by law, men are committing these abominable crimes day after day. Do you think they lack courage? In West Bengal, the rate of women abuse is higher than the other states. There is no reason that we should assume that the passengers in the said bus are not involved in such pernicious acts like beating their wives, sexual abuse, or women trafficking. No reason to think that they consider sexual harassment a heinous crime. Further, I believe that these people had mentally sided with those youths who perpetrated the crime. They were truly disappointed as it was not feasible for them to participate physically in the sexual abuse of that victim because of the limited space inside the moving bus. Had there been open space for all, they would have delightfully taken part in sexual harassment, and if there was provision for gang rape, they would have wilfully participated in that.

The epithets like coward, timid and so on are used to cover up the villainy. These abuses are almost like the honeyed calls of a mother to her darling children. "My little son is so coward that he can't sleep alone. My daughter has little courage to go out on the streets alone." Or, like a friend speaking to another: "You rascal have no courage at all! The girl, so sexy, voluntarily came to you but you desisted from even touching her?" These honeyed invectives are in fact signs of admiration. Therefore, the people who are abusing the bus passengers with these epithets for remaining silent will do better to keep their mouth shut. They should realize that it is a question of morality which is lacking in most of us. They should realize that as it is unjustified to heckle men because they are men, similarly it is equally unjustified to heckle women because they are women. People are oblivious of the fact that as freedom is the birthright of all men, it is the birthright of all women as well. Women are not incomplete; they are also complete human beings and deserve all the admiration and dignity of a human being. For sheer fun and pleasure, no man has the right to pass comments of sexual hints towards a passing woman and humiliate or outrage her.

Attempt is now being made to net the victim. The latter has escaped from the bus. The loudspeakers now blare: "The victim, wherever you are, come out of your hiding. Tell the police what the naughty chaps had done with you. Unless you come out, until the people of the state have a glimpse of your cute face, their hearts will not be content. If you don't, other victims also will not learn the art of coming out. Then it'll be an irrecoverable damage to the civilization."

But the victim is ignoring the loudspeaker. The tune of the piper does not enter the ears of the victim. A combing operation is on in search of the victim. Many are thrilled at the thought that the victim will narrate in detail in the court how she was heckled. So the girl is wanted to show, at least once, her celebrated face to the public.

But why she should respond to this call? Is not enough is enough? Where were they when she was crying in the bus? Everybody saw her cries, her pains, her lamentations and her helplessness. Now, why will she come out to show her face and appearance? Is there any basic difference between those people in the bus, and the people at large? Who will give her the guarantee that people will not disgrace her again? She has seen enough of the mobile court in the bus in which the jury was sitting silently. Does she need to see another court?

The gentlemen say that this girl too has gone into hibernation like the one for whom the police sergeant Bapi Sen was murdered. Some people are accusing women for their habit of escaping from the reality. As a matter of fact, these girls have learnt to the bone that if they come out in the public, they will run the risk of being further sexually abused. If they dare to bring the culprits to book, they will invite renewed wrath of the abusers. The real-life experience has taught them that if they file suits in the court, they will suffer, not the culprits. Girls have lost faith in them who talk of protecting them and invariably fail to do so. In the name of sympathy, they actually make the girls bleed. Despite all tall talks, girls are without security. Religion, culture, state, society, family—nowhere there is an iota of security for women.

It is known to women that once people come to know about the victim, they will be crazy to see her face. The culprits who are still at large will get a second opportunity to see their victim. The local teasers will point to her saying, 'Look, there goes the victim of eve-teasing!' Men will say, though there were scores of other girls in the bus, why did the boys single her out? She must have provoked them.

The girl is hiding in order to save her from further humiliation. She must be regretting the foolish reaction of Jagannath and Subhendu. She has taken it for granted that she has to swallow this kind of humiliation and torture for the rest of her life everywhere—at home, outside, in the bus, train, autorickshaw, markets, crowded places—just because she is a girl. So she does not want to humiliate herself again saying, 'I was sexually abused.' Girls wisely save themselves from double, triple humiliations.

They say I am too bold. Yet had I been in place of that girl, I would not have disclosed my identity before the misogynistic people of society that I was the girl in the bus.

***

43

Why Not Feminine
Names for Top Posts?

The higher posts are meant for men. So in Bengali, a masculine suffix is pervasively used in the names of these posts. That suffix is '*pati*' (lord or husband), e.g., '*bhupati*' (landlord), '*rashtrapati*' (president), '*sabhapati*' (chairman), '*dalapati*' (team leader). The wives were confined to the household in the past, and so are they now. They did not have any access to education, so is it even today. Now, in order to give facelift to the extremity of gender discrimination, and to introduce a reservation of sorts, suddenly the married women 'going to the offices with pen in their hands'* are made to face such official posts which they hardly had the right to hold. Now, after putting 'untouchable' or 'minority' persons in the post of the President, India decided to put a woman—the best

---

* One among many satirical descriptions given by educated Bengali men against women education.

untouchable and minority is of course the women—in that post, assuming that for following such liberal policy, it would command great name and honour among the nations of the world. A woman would be the 'lord' of the nation. But a lord or *pati* is a man. The post is meant for the males, then why should a woman chair it? Many would disagree with the idea that a post meant for males should undergo a change of name if a woman is elected for it. There are quite a few intellectuals among them and also some distinguished feminists. But I feel as at the time of creation of these posts it never occurred to any man that both men and women have right to hold these posts, there must be a sort of penitence now. Either gendered names of posts must cease to exist, or other posts distinctly for women must be created. Is it not better that the name of posts must indicate both sexes, irrespective of gender distinction? Many people are not ready for this; they want the gendered names of posts to continue, offering the reason that it is not 'practical' as it would require to change all things like stamp pad. Only the convention is 'practical'. Accidentally a woman has come to occupy a post that normally belonged to men, so therefore the old name should continue to be used. Expensive, troublesome and such other reasons are forwarded by patriarchal men, as well as by women who are in favour of patriarchy.

I do not support this. The additional expenditure and troubles are very much needed to be borne. Even many undue expenses are borne by the state. This expense is for the sake of an epoch-making change for the sake of humanity. And the costs of changing the name of the posts in the official documents is not so much high that Indian Government would not be able to meet up the expense. So many cities have undergone change of names. Were they not unnecessary? When Bombay became Mumbai, Madras Chennai, and Calcutta Kolkata, is it that only change of seals and pads suffice? A thousand of other changes are required. But this is no romantic nationalism as change of the names of cities; it is a movement for the sake of humanity against age-old celebration of gender distinction fostered by patriarchy.

Gender bias of society would make itself prominent day-by-day unless the idea that humanity must endow men and women with equal status is rooted in society, in state, in man's views and thoughts.

Those who claim that *Rashtrapati* is only the name of a post and both men and women are entitled for this post', to them I repeat that it is, of course, the name of a post but the name of a male-post. A woman can hold the position, undoubtedly, but even then it remains a post for the males. History, linguistics, patriarchy, everything would affirm this.

Movements for gender-free words have taken place in other foreign countries as well. Fireman is now called fire-fighter. A barman is called a bartender. A steward or a stewardess is now called a flight attendant. A mailman is a mail carrier; chairman has turned into chairperson or chair. Use of singular 'they' has been introduced in place of 'he' and 'she'. In Europe and America, in educational institutions as well as in business organizations, use of gendered words has been restricted. This is a very good move. Those who are not in favour of this, they are not supporters of human rights, of modernism, and of evolutionary progress.

If protest is raised against use of gendered words, the opposition would rush to complain that 'such cosmetic changes will not bring any effective change in the patriarchal system'. They would say that 'unnecessary torture is being inflicted on language'. They would say, there are a lot more serious problems in our country and attention must be given to them.

In case of amendments or corrections made in favour of women, there has never been dearth of opposition. But those who support human rights know that it should be maintained everywhere even in spoken tongue. Even a minor word has great significance. And if it is something like the Bengali word *rashtrapati*, then it has to have great significance.

. For women, the post may be renamed as *rashtranetri* in Bengali, or some thing like that. If a gender-irrespective term is to be used, then *rashtrapradhan* is a good word. A linguist is to determine which word would be most appropriate. I only say that for the Bengali term *rashtrapati*, there should be either a gender-specific term or a gender-neutral term.

If this post, from the very beginning, would have been called in Bengali, *rashtranetri* instead of *rashtrapati*, and the men would have been diplomatically restricted from holding this post, would the men then accept without protest the designation of *rashtranetri*? No. If the Bengali term *jharudaar* is replaced by *jharudaarni*, will the male sweepers tolerate that? Similarly, if someone as important as *rashtrapati* is called *rashtranetri*, it would not be tolerated. It is thought that since the post of the President normally belongs to males, for a woman an opportunity to hold the position and be called *rashtrapati* is not only perfect, but attractive and prestigious as well. In this society men are always on top, so when a woman achieves a 'man's post', it is considered to be her promotion in status. If a woman cross-dresses, she is looked upon as smart. Many think it is modern to use *sampadak/lekhak* (in English, editor/author) instead of *sampadika/lekhika* (in English, woman editor/authoress). The word 'actress' has now become obsolete in favour of actor. What can be its opposite? If all the famous actors are made to be called actresses? Will they allow it? There's no question of this, rather they would laugh at the proposition. One of Madonna's songs come to my mind:

> *'Girls can wear jeans*
> *And cut their hair short*
> *Wear shirts and boots*
> *'Cause it's okay to be a boy*
> *But for a boy to look like a girl is degrading*
> *'Cause you think that being a girl is degrading'*

If a boy cross-dresses, it is demeaning for him. If a man holds a woman's post, it is seen as his degradation in status. Such is society. Under such social circumstance, when a woman President is not designated as *rashtranetri or rashtrapradhan*, but continued to be referred to as *rashtrapoti* in Bengali, this is nothing but a conspiracy to maintain the post as a masculine one. If a woman is given a man's post, it is looked upon as something very smart and honourable, as if it is a promotion for her. No one can doubt that such views are extremely patriarchal.

Only the nation knows how much time it would require to elect another woman President, for the second time, when it needed 60 long years to do it for the first time! There is so much of male domination here that no one can dare make the post-names free from masculine reference. The men feel very comfortable with the male posts. Males are on the top everywhere, be it in the social structure, and even more in the political structure. Man is the ultimate supreme of all beings, with nothing else to supersede him. Although the women don't understand, the men definitely do, that this politics of offering male posts to the women will lead women to nowhere but rather harm them.

To be raised in status by occupying men's posts is no achievement at all. Rather, to acquire a distinct identity through separation of female posts from male posts is something substantial. This society does not recognize women's distinctive identity. This 'no' should be challenged. Is there nothing in a name? There's a lot in a name. It can make a great difference as one's own existence is acknowledged by one's name. Is this insignificant? If a woman does not get recognition being a woman and holding a woman's post, if for that she has to be like a man and get hold of a man's post, then it cannot be honourable for her. Rather, it is extremely degrading.

Some are of the opinion that the Bengali word *rashtranetri* is new and would be unacceptable for people. This is not true. So long there had been no Bengali term to mean girlhood. To refer to it, one would require to use the word *chhelebela* (that is boyhood in English). But as soon as I introduced the word *meyebela* (in English, girlhood) in the 80s, people quickly picked it up. Creation of new posts calls for an increase in the number of posts. How can there be new posts without new initiatives? How will people's mentality change? If there's no change in mentality it will not result in any change of post.

***

44

A Gender-neutral Bengali Language Required

The people who are supposed to liberate Bengali language from poverty and discrimination and enrich its resources are certainly wise, experienced and knowledgeable persons. I can guess they are mostly men. But I do not believe they all carry patriarchal mentality. I appeal to them as well as the people in general to promote and campaign for a Bengali language that is free from gender discrimination. In the civilized countries , where women are treated as human beings, languages are free from gender inequalities. If initiative is not taken to eradicate discrimination in Bengali language, Bengali women will continue to be heckled in the field of culture, law, tradition and mannerism. I'm going to cite some examples of changes made in English language to free it from gender discrimination.

Earlier form	Present form
Man	Human being
Mankind	Human kind, humanity
Man's achievement	Human achievement
Manfully	Valiantly
Manpower	Work force, human energy, human resources
Man made	Human induced
Brotherhood of man	Human fellowship, human kinship
Brotherly	Friendly
Man and wife	Husband and wife
Businessman	Business manager
Cameraman	Photographer, camera operator, camera crew
Craftsman	Crafts worker, artisan
Craftsmanship	Craft, craft skills
Fellow countryman	Compatriot
Foreman	Supervisor
Gentleman's agreement	Honourable agreement
Landlord	Owner, proprietor
Lay man	Lay person, non-professional
Ombudsman	Mediator
Policeman	Police, police officer
Salesman	Sales assistant
Spokesman	Spokesperson
Sportsman	Sports person/sports woman (Occasionally)
Workman like	Well-executed

John and Mary have full time jobs; he helps her with the house work.	John and Mary have full-time jobs, they share housework.
Transport will be provided for delegates and their wives.	Transport will be provided for delegates and their spouses or persons accompanying them.
The doctor... he	Doctors... they
The nurse... she	Nurses... they
Woman doctor, male nurse	Doctor, nurse
Mothering	Parenting, nurturing, child rearing
Housewife	Home-maker
Forefathers	Ancestors
Founding fathers	Founders
Woman driver	Driver
Gunman	Shooter
The common man	The average person, ordinary people

If Bengali language is made free from gender bias (and if required gender-specific), it will assume a civilized form; otherwise, it will remain as patriarchal as it has been for ages. First of all, the lexicon must be revised accordingly.

Men and women are physically different from each other—this cannot be denied. I'm not talking about changing their intrinsic qualities. The role of men and women varies from society to society. Their economic, social, political and cultural faculties differ from each other. Their roles in society are classified. This classification has been deliberately done by men. Women were debarred by men from taking lead roles in socio-political and economic spheres. So when one speaks of gender equality, many people wrongly apprehend that attempt is being made to deny the physical difference between the two sexes. No, what is demanded is that both men and women should enjoy equal share of rights and privileges.

The word *abala* in Bengali is used to denote a woman who is supposed to be weak. Then why not use the masculine gender *abal* for men who are weak and feeble? The Bengali renderings of words like chaste, unchaste, concubine, strumpet, whore, prostitute, fallen woman, kept woman, courtesan, bawd, tart, hustler, moil, are all feminine in gender. I would demand either for the mandatory use of masculine gender of these words in Bengali or scrapping of these words from the vocabulary.

The words 'virgin' and 'chaste' are associated with females only. For males no such words are required. I know it is not possible to impose some new words into a vocabulary. But if people become conscious, new words and sentences will come into use. Male domination has turned Bengali language anti-feminine in character. The commonly used ugly invectives, slangs and elements of sexual innuendo in male conversations are anti-feminine. The society bursts into laughter after humiliating women!

At every step of life, I have to face the onslaught of patriarchal language. Suppose Subrata invites me to his home, and then I decide to go there with my friend Amit. Now, Subrata would at once speak to Amit on telephone to tell him to escort me to his house. Amit does not know Subrata's address. My chauffeur may know it. I can also read the route map to reach the destination.

Amit has no role to play here. He is in the car listening to the stereo all the way. It's me or my driver who finds out Subrata's residence. At Subrata's residence, everyone will thank Amit for taking the trouble of escorting me safely to the destination.

'Who escorted you here?' people normally ask a woman who has come to a party alone. But nobody asks a man the same question. The belief that women cannot travel alone has influenced the language.

In day-to-day life, language is reflecting the domination of the males; but no one seems to have taken note of it.

'Subrata has gone out with his wife just now.' Instead of this sentence, it could have been said: 'Subrata and Rituparna have just gone out.'

Practically, there is no standard Bengali version of the expression 'They are making love.' In colloquial Bengali, they say: 'the boy is doing on the girl.' There is no involvement of two persons in this expression. One is active and the other person is passive.

Poet and woman-poet are used in Bengali. But I think the word poet should be used to denote both man and woman poets. If the word woman-poet can be used, then why not male poet? Similarly, take the example of male journalist and female journalist. The word journalist should denote either a man or a woman.

There are certain advantages in making Bengali language free from gender discrimination. In English, he and she, him and her distinguishes between males and females. But in Bengali, a common word is used as personal pronoun that denotes both male and female.

It is a common practice in Bengali to say 'husband-wife', 'Uttam-Suchitra', and so on. Why not reverse it?

The question of reformation of language is important because language is not only the reflection of our mentality, our language can mould our mentality as well. If the constant use of a language builds the impression that women are weak, parasites and vile creatures, it will go into the mindset of the people that women are really so.

The world is getting modernized. People are increasingly becoming aware of equality and equal rights. Women are breaking open the shackles of slavery. There is a gradual evolution of human's thoughts and ideologies. Then why should Bengali language lag behind? The more it will be purified, the more society will be civilized.

45

The Story of Sankha and Sindur

Married women should not come to the school with *sankhu* (a bangle made of white shell) and *sindur* (vermilion), and should not gossip with unmarried girls about their conjugal life: This was the instruction issued by the authority of a school in Murshidabad. This instigated the people and the media to burst into loud protest. This is a fatwa against Hindu religion. The authority tried to argue that if such narration of spicy stories about conjugal lives attracts the unmarried ones towards married life, they may ignore their studies and go for marriage. It did not cut any ice with anyone, and the authority was compelled to withdraw its instruction.

On the other hand, the villagers of Guma in north 24 parganas thrashed Rima Bouddha and threw her out of the village. Her crime was that even after marriage she was neither wearing *sankha* nor *sindur*. She was not using those as she was a

Buddhist, but the villagers issued a fatwa that a married woman would have to use those, otherwise she would not be allowed to live in the village. So Rina Bouddha had to leave the village with her husband Birendra Bouddha. She wants to live a secured life in her village, but the administration has failed to assure her of her security till now.

There are many stories of *sankha* and *sindur*.* Often Saptami comes to my house to spend some time with me. She was born in the Sunderbans and now lives at Sonarpur. The year a flood washed away their hut, her father left the village with his wife and 11 children and settled in Sonarpur. Saptami was then a child of seven months. Keeping Saptami seated on the floor, her mother used to serve people as a domestic help. Saptami too has worked as a domestic help from a very tender age. She was married at the age of about 12 or 13. Her husband never loved her. She served everybody in the in-laws' house, and even then her husband and in-laws used to beat her. Still she stayed there as it was the house of her husband. One day her husband bet her severely and threw her out of the house along with her two little daughters. Fifteen years have passed thereafter. In these 15 years, her husband has not contacted her. He never bothered to enquire about the two girls; never ever gave her any money. She had gone through very hard days financially. She has survived without food or being half-fed, and have managed to bring up those two children. Years ago, her husband married again. But Saptami still uses *sankha* and *sindur*, and wears an iron bangle also. I asked her: "That

---

* These are the symbols of a married Hindu woman in Bengal.

person made you suffer so much, beat you, threw you out from his house, has not contacted you in these 15 years… and you'll not go back to him ever, neither would he accept you… then why are you still using *sankha* and *sindur*?"

Saptami answered, "We cannot give up these after using it once."

"Why are you not divorcing him?"

"In our community, the women cannot divorce our husbands."

"Who said this? Of course, they can. Your husband has married again without divorcing you. Do you know that in your community one cannot marry again before getting divorced?"

Saptami could not get me properly. I again explained to her that according to Hindu laws women can divorce their husbands and no one has the right to marry again before getting divorced. Saptami was not aware of such things. She named quite a few men who were living with two-three wives.

"Where?" I asked her.

She answered, "In Sonarpur, Subashgram, Sunderbans."

I have seen when Saptami wants to make me believe in a certain thing, she touches the *sankha* with the other hand and says, "*Didi*, I swear by my husband…"

For her, the *sankha* is a sacred thing. She wants to wear it. The day she would have to break it, will be a fearsome day for her.

I laugh and tell her, "Your husband has never enquired about you. Never helped you in your bad days. Your children do not know who their father is. What's the difference between whether that man is alive or dead?"

"Wherever he is, I want he should live on," said Saptami.

"Why?" I asked.

"I want to die with *sankha* and *sindur*."

If a married woman dies before her husband she dies with *sankha* and *sindur*, and then she goes to heaven. Women like Saptami are all about us. I know of many such women who use *sankha* and *sindur* with utmost joy, though their husbands have married again, do not care for them, or beat them to break their limbs, or take away their hard-earned money to squander it on booze.

"If you do not use *sankh-sindur*, you may meet someone, a good man, may get married to him… may get a chance to start a new life with him."

Saptami started laughing. She said, "No, *didi*. We get married only once. We can have only one husband. You are talking of a good man. No, we cannot trust anyone. Initially, they may appear good, but ultimately they all will be like my husband."

Another day she said, "We have to have *sankha* and *sindur* to protect ourselves from bad people. These are the symbols that show we are not unidentified luggage."

I understood that these symbols provide security to women. Though there exists no husband for a woman like Saptami, she takes shelter in *sankha-sindur* so that the wolves and vultures do not pounce upon her.

But I do not believe that *sankha-sindur* can provide any security to women. Men who come to devour a woman, to pounce upon her for raping her, who come with evil intention cannot be resisted by *sankha-sindur*.

I feel sorry for Saptami and other hundred thousand women like Saptami. The woman lives alone in a hut. Whether she succeeds to manage or not two square meals, she goes overboard to arrange for money to offer puja for her husband. What security do *sankha* and *sindur* provide her? I asked her whether anyone has tried to dishonour her.

"Many have done that," said Saptami. "Always trying to do that."

"Then of what use?" I was about to tell her, but I did not. She herself said, "I cannot sleep well in the night. I keep a cleaver near my bed. Whenever I hear a rap on the door, I go near it with the sickle. Come on, either you live or I."

"You are so courageous," I say in admiration.

"If I lacked in courage, people would have cut me into pieces. No one helps me with a little money. I get up in the early morning and after eating watered rice I catch a crowded train. After serving so many houses, I return in the night. I have courage and that is why I have saved money bit by bit and bought a little land to make a hut. People have slandered me like anything. I never paid any heed to those. Why should I? Would they feed me even once?"

I ask, "Then why do you bother about what would they say if you do not use *sankha-sindur*? Let them say. How does it matter to you if they think you are an unidentified luggage? If you say that then someone may try to touch you, may tease you, may pounce upon you, so what? You have your cleaver. What are you afraid of?"

Sapatami's eyes reflect a different kind of fear. The fear of challenging the mighty age-old superstition. Apart from Saptami, thousands of other Saptamis too have this fear.

Poor women do certain things that the rich educated women cannot even dream of. Women like Saptami are not aware of the laws, and so they do not follow those. But they uproot any challenge coming in their way of securing their food. They do not care for what the others say. They live alone with fierce courage and strength. No one helps them a bit. They struggle hard, even for every grain of food they earn. They have not gone to school, do not know even a letter. They know how to board a running train. They know how to save themselves if someone grasp their shoulder. They know how to abuse them. They know how to break the hand that tries to snatch their money. They know how to slice the man who enters the hut in the dark of the night. What they do not know is how to break the shell-bangle, how to rub off the vermilion from their foreheads. Most women are still in the shackles of superstition, even the vehemently bold ones.

***

46

Religion and Women's Rights Cannot Coexist

Women's rights, liberty, human rights, humanity, liberal thoughts, right to expression, democracy, and secular lifestyle cannot coexist with religion, fundamentalism, religious fundamentalism, religious laws, rule of religion and so on. The conflict between these two sets of attitudes to life has been age-old. It started from the time when religion came into being. It is quite obvious that if I'm vociferous about the rights of women, the religious fanatics will attack me. Many often ask me: 'Why do you provoke them? If you cross a limit, it is natural that they will pounce on you, announce fatwas on you or kill you.' It simply means let the women be deprived of their own rights by the fundamentalists, let fundamentalism create terror in society, let it bind women in the chains of slavery, let it imprison women in the dungeon of darkness, but women should not protest. Otherwise, they will invite the wrath of fundamentalists who will be angry, will abuse you or throw stones. That will create chaos in the society, which can never be allowed to happen.

There was a time when society was controlled purely by religion. The age was known as the Dark Age. The Christians burnt many women to death in the name of witch hunting. The Hindus too burnt women alive forcing them to be Sati. Polygamy prevailed among the males and women were deprived of the share of property and human rights. They were just treated as sex slaves and as instruments for production of male babies. In Islam, though women were not burnt alive, they were treated as sex slaves and as property of their male counterparts just like in other religious communities. Several philosophers, rationalists and liberal thinkers in different ages criticized the rule of religion and spoke in favour of gender equality and social justice. In all ages and in all societies, they came under attack. Even Galileo, Giordano Bruno, Vidyasagar, Rammohan Roy, who had tried to enlighten the Dark Ages, were not spared from this. There had never been dearth of men seeking the heads of the social reformers. There is no dearth of them now either.

Due to untiring labour of the rationalists, gradually moral and mass education spread and religion was separated from the state in lands of non-Muslims. But, most of the Muslim areas are still lagging behind. The capitalist societies have been exploiting the Muslim societies for long. They were able to meet their selfish ends by drowning the common people into the ocean of ignorance and superstitions. The autocracy, vested interests and short-sightedness of the Islamic rulers have kept the Muslim societies a light year away from the civilization. Human rights, humanity, rights of women, democracy, and freedom of speech are almost non-existent in these societies. And what is happening in these societies is influencing the minority Muslim citizens in the rest of the world. Instead of becoming secular, people are growing up as fundamentalists. Besides, the bombing of the Muslim states by the arrogant superpower further misguided the youths to follow the path of fundamentalism. The fall of communism also confused the people across the globe, encouraging them to take refuge in religion.

It is quite impossible to combat the monstrous force of fundamentalism without a revolution or a mass upsurge. The more the people will shrivel in fear of the fundamental forces, the more acute shall be the crisis of civilization day-by-day. Like democracy, human rights cannot be imposed from without. Before enjoying the fruits of democracy and human rights, the people must be well prepared. Consciousness is the pre-condition to preparedness. Several thinkers and social reformers have from time to time tried to create such basic consciousness among the people. Personally, I also try to do similar things through my writings.

Being born in a Muslim majority country, I saw from a close quarter the nature of control Islamic laws and dictates had on women. Again, as I grew up in a multicultural society, I also witnessed the injustice inflicted by other religions on their women. I am a very ordinary person. I studied medicine. I was supposed to lead a solvent life after graduating in medicine. But forgoing everything as such and braving risks in life, I started to speak vociferously on the rights of women in a society dominated by misogynists, male chauvinists, religious zealots and impatient fundamentalists. Why? Is it out of sheer fun?

Or, is it because I believe that I owe some responsibilities to purge the society of its evils? Someone must stand against the blackguards who perpetrate misrule in society. Some people are always there who are uncompromising, who wage a relentless battle against injustice.

Nurturing the dreams of healthy, equal and beautiful society, I waged a relentless battle against religious fundamentalism, superstitions and male dominance, and that forced me to live my life in banishment for the last 13 years. Had I yielded to their condition of keeping mum, I could have returned to my native land. I would not have to run from one country to another in search of shelter. I would not have to live a miserable life in isolation from my friends and relatives. I courted a life of misery only because I wanted to write the things which few dared to write; I wanted to traverse the path which very few dared to travel.

I keep on saying that I am not alone in this battle against fundamentalism. It engages all people who have faith in free-thinking, right to expression and personal freedom. This battle is between truth and falsehood, reason and irrationality, old and modern, civilization and savagery, equality and inequality, knowledge and ignorance, and progress and regression.

Time and again orthodox male chauvinists and fundamentalists attacked me. Why? They announced fatwas against me. Why? They fixed the price of my head. Why? Surely because I have been able to stir the hornet's nest. If I write for the rights of women, it is obvious that the antagonists of women rights will not be happy with me.

Attack does not necessarily mean physical attack only. It can be made in the form of propaganda and character assassination and campaigns against somebody. After every attack on me, the intellectuals or progressive organizations of artists, writers, etc., had condemned the attack on me, but also clarified that they did not support my viewpoint. When this happens, I feel a strong urge in me to know from them as to which aspect of my ideology they do not agree to. I write to fight for four ideals: Human right, Women's rights, Humanism and Secularism. Of these four ideals, which one are they opposed to?

Some fundamentalists masquerading as progressives have often alerted me that I should not provoke anyone or cross the limit. They advise me to be restrained and cautious while writing so that the fundamentalists are not annoyed, not provoked to take out processions on the streets. Some are of the opinion that I do all these things deliberately to acquire popularity by provoking the fundamentalists to go berserk. Some others even go to the extent of saying that I cannot write either prose or poetry. I am, according to them, not a litterateur. I only make comments to provoke the fundamentalists. Therefore, there exists enough logic for the fundamentalists to attack me. Some even say that I have not actually written anything on women's education, health and economic independence, and that I do not want anything called women's freedom. What I actually want is sexual freedom of women. That is why, they say, the fundamentalists attack me. The people who accuse me of these things have earned a good deal of fame as intellectuals. Their false and slanderous campaign against me is actually intended to complement and prop up the attacks of the fundamentalists on me.

Besides religious fanatics, a monstrous power is nakedly trying to choke my voice. Even those senseless religious fanatics who are members of the legislative assemblies or the heads of the law board openly declare that they are willing to court death sentence after killing me. People vehemently condemn them. But those clever men who are known as progressive people come out with their proposition, feigning wisdom, that I should not cross a limit or say certain things that hurt the sentiments of others' faith or religion. These people have a strong influence over the general masses, and are basically twice more dangerous than the fundamentalists. A fatwa to 'be within limits' is more dangerous than the fatwa to 'fix the price' of one's head. A fatwa to fix the price of my head may lead to my killing one day, but 'to be within limits' means I am supposed to keep my mouth shut for the rest of my life. I think the pains and sufferings for a long duration are more terrible than a day's suffering.

If I open my mouth against religion and fundamentalism, the pious or fundamentalists accuse me of crossing the limit. The peace-loving litterateurs, who subscribe to the theory that fundamentalism and women's rights can coexist without confronting each other, too opine that I am crossing the limit. They will blame the women if there arises any conflict. They give advice to encourage and pamper the venomous snake called fundamentalism. They cannot see that one snake is begetting lakhs of snakes. For them, being within the limits is tantamount to a life shrunk in fear with mouth shut, and breathes bated.

I'm happy to think that I am not alone in my struggle. I'm walking in the procession of those innumerable people who are rationalist, liberated from religion, and are humanitarian in their approach. As an individual, I am tiny, but together we are not small. Perhaps, someday the enemies will easily crush me. But they will not be able to crush all of us. I have spent every moment of my life in fear of death. I will die in peace when I shall know that women have been able to identify religion and fundamentalism as their greatest enemies. That day I'll die happily when I shall know that fundamentalism has ceased to exist; that women are living in dignity, with full rights as a human being, educated and self-reliant.

In the absence of the religious fanatics, women do not need to wear *burqas*, cover their heads with veils and keep indoors and shun the company of men other than their husbands and male relatives. I'll die peacefully knowing that no fundamentalist exists anymore to issue diktats that a woman should be slave of her husband; should comply with the whims and caprices of her husband, bear tortures without protest, and oblige him by giving birth to as many children as he desires. Or to proclaim, you are nobody's heir, your life is not for you but for somebody else's comforts and favours; you are not a human being, you are a vile worm of hell and the door to inferno.

***